690.0684 RA

RISK ANALYSIS
IN PROJECT MANAGEMENT

Avril Robarts LRC

Liverpool John Moores University

LIVERPOOL JMU LIBRARY

3 1111 00671 5872

OTHER TITLES FROM E & FN SPON

Architectural Management
M.P. Nicholson

Introduction to Building Procurement Systems
J.W.E. Masterman

Construction Conflicts Management and Resolution
P. Fenn and R. Gameson

Construction Contracts
Law and management
J.R. Murdoch and W. Hughes

A Concise Introduction to Engineering Economics
P. Cassimatis

The Idea of Building
S. Groák

Investment, Procurement and Performance in Construction
P. Venmore-Rowland, P. Brandon and T. Mole

The Management of Quality in Construction
J.L. Ashford

Management, Quality and Economics in Building
P. Brandon and A. Bezelga

Profitable Practice Management
For the construction professional
P. Barrett

Project Management Demystified
Today's tools and techniques
G. Reiss

Spon's Budget Estimating Handbook
Spain and Partners

Value Management in Design and Construction
S. Male and J. Kelly

Effective Speaking
Communicating in speech
C. Turk

Effective Writing
Improving scientific, technical and business communication
2nd Edition
C. Turk and J. Kirkman

Good Style
Writing for science and technology
J. Kirkman

Journals

Construction Management and Economics
Editors: R. Bon and W. Hughes'

Building Research and Information
Editor: A. Kirk

For more information on these and other titles please contact: The Promotion Department, E & FN Spon, 2–6 Boundary Row, London, SE1 8HN. Telephone (0)71 865 0066.

RISK ANALYSIS IN PROJECT MANAGEMENT

JOHN RAFTERY

Professor of Construction Economics
University of Greenwich, Dartford, UK

E & FN SPON

An Imprint of Chapman & Hall
London · Glasgow · New York · Tokyo · Melbourne · Madras

Published by E & FN Spon, an imprint of Chapman & Hall, 2–6 Boundary Row, London SE1 8HN, UK

Chapman & Hall, 2–6 Boundary Row, London SE1 8HN, UK

Blackie Academic & Professional, Wester Cleddens Road, Bishopbriggs, Glasgow G64 2NZ, UK

Chapman & Hall Inc., One Penn Plaza, 41st Floor, New York NY 10119, USA

Chapman & Hall Japan, Thomson Publishing Japan, Hirakawacho Nemoto Building, 6F, 1-7-11 Hirakawa-cho, Chiyoda-ku, Tokyo 102, Japan

Chapman & Hall Australia, Thomas Nelson Australia, 102 Dodds Street, South Melbourne, Victoria 3205, Australia

Chapman & Hall India, R. Seshadri, 32 Second Main Road, CIT East, Madras 600 035, India

First edition 1994

© 1994 John Raftery

Typeset in 10½/13½ Sabon by Acorn Bookwork, Salisbury, Wiltshire

Printed in Great Britain by
St Edmundsbury Press Limited, Bury St Edmunds, Suffolk

ISBN 0 419 18420 1

Apart from any fair dealing for the purposes of research or private study, or criticism or review, as permitted under the UK Copyright Designs and Patents Act, 1988, this publication may not be reproduced, stored, or transmitted, in any form or by any means, without the prior permission in writing of the publishers, or in the case of reprographic reproduction only in accordance with the terms of the licences issued by the Copyright Licensing Agency in the UK, or in accordance with the terms of licences issued by the appropriate Reproduction Rights Organization outside the UK. Enquiries concerning reproduction outside the terms stated here should be sent to the publishers at the London address printed on this page.

The publisher makes no representation, express or implied, with regard to the accuracy of the information contained in this book and cannot accept any legal responsibility or liability for any errors or omissions that may be made.

A catalogue record for this book is available from the British Library

Library of Congress Cataloging-in-Publication data

Raftery, John.
    Risk analysis in project management / John Raftery.—1st ed.
      p.   cm.
    Includes index.
    ISBN 0-419-18420-1 (alk. paper)
      1. Industrial project management.   2. Risk management.   I. Title.
    T56.8.R34   1994
    658.4′04—dc20
                                 93-32191
                                     CIP

∞ Printed on permanent acid-free text paper, manufactured in accordance with ANSI/NISO Z39.48-1992 (Permanence of Paper).

TO MEADHBH,
FEARGHUS AND TOM

CONTENTS

PREFACE

The principal objective of this book is to demystify the subject of risk analysis. The focus of the book is on the **analysis** rather than the **management** of risk. This is a practical text which minimizes jargon, mathematics and academic references. The text contains descriptions of the nature of risk and risk attitude, and psychological aspects of forecasting construction price and time. Techniques of analysis are described together with an assessment of their strengths and weaknesses. Case studies and worked examples are presented to show how they may be used in practice to carry out sophisticated risk appraisal on a range of projects covering building and major civil engineering and infrastructure work. The worked examples demonstrate how risk may be dealt with by construction clients and contractors. The emphasis of the book is not on model or checklist approaches to risk analysis; the book provides an opportunity for professionals to learn how to think systematically about project risks and to develop a maturity of judgement regarding project risk analysis. There is no intention here to replace judgement with analysis; the opposite is the case. Risk analysis enables decision makers to improve the quality of their judgements by providing more realistic information on which to base decisions.

The text is based on a series of risk analysis presentations and workshops over the past ten years to international construction clients, consultants and contractors in Europe, Scandinavia and South East Asia. Most of the examples are based on real projects.

The book is aimed at practitioners (architects, engineers, project managers, quantity and building surveyors) who need a quick, easy to assimilate introduction to the field and at students on a range of construction and property-related courses who may be taking options in risk management. A recent RICS report on the future of the quantity surveying (QS) profession has indicated risk analysis as one of the new high value-added services which QS firms will need to offer to their clients in order to survive and prosper into the late 1990s. This is a practical text which aims to enable the reader to be brought quickly up to date on the subject. There is therefore sufficient material for the construction professional to feel confident about undertaking systematic risk analysis; and sufficient also to enable the reader to decide when it is necessary to call for specialist advice.

ACKNOWLEDGEMENTS

For such a short book, I owe many debts. I worked closely on some of the ideas with Dr Stephen Mak, now at Hong Kong Polytechnic. Stephen coded the software that was used on some of the cases described in Chapters 5 and 6, and drafted the questions used in the personal bias section of Chapter 3. Randy Yu, my colleague at Greenwich, wrote up the case study of the Thames Bridge based on my amendments to one of our consultancies and also supplied me with the Goh Kee Contracting Company example used in Chapter 6. My colleague Professor David Wills supplied the material for Figure 1.7. I am grateful to my consultancy clients, who wish to remain anonymous, in Finland, South East Asia, Washington and London. In the same context I have relied on the support of Jenny Lynch, who runs our consultancy office, and Sue Lee, who produced the artwork for the diagrams. Tim DeLap helped with the St Alfege's project which I ran on our Master's programme in 1989. Maxine Davis supplied the figures in Tables 5.1–5.3. Others who have helped directly or indirectly include John Limpert now in North Carolina, Derek Drew and David Picken in Hong Kong, Frank Grogan and Jim Foley in London, Anders Ekman and Seppo Nilsson in Helsinki and Professor Bo-Christer Bjork now at the Royal Institute of Technology in Stockholm. I received detailed comments, criticisms and suggestions on an earlier draft of the text from Kieran Raftery and from my colleague Dr Hilary Davies. All of these people were responsible for improvements to this work. There is still room for improvement, and for any errors or inaccuracies blame me, not them.

John Raftery
Greenwich, September 1993

CHAPTER 1

RISKS AND UNCERTAINTIES IN PROJECTS

1.1 THE PURPOSE OF THIS BOOK

1.2 RISK AND UNCERTAINTY: DEFINITIONS

1.3 RISK EXPOSURE AND RISK ATTITUDE

1.4 RISK IN PROJECTS
    1.4.1 Project heterogeneity
    1.4.2 Budgeting and tender price forecasting
    1.4.3 Project-based sources of risk
    1.4.4 External risks

1.5 AN OVERVIEW OF RISK MANAGEMENT
    1.5.1 Risk identification
    1.5.2 Risk analysis
    1.5.3 Risk response

1.6 RISK ANALYSIS: ADVANTAGES AND LIMITATIONS

1.7 SUMMARY

*This is not a speculative game at all. Our objective is
not to avoid risk but to recognise it, price it and sell it.*

Tony Ryan, chairman of Guiness Peat Aviation Ltd,
quoted in the *Observer*, 14 June 1992, p. 49

1.1 THE PURPOSE OF THIS BOOK

Someone once said 'Most books, on most subjects are too long'.
Here is a short book on risk analysis. The primary objective of this
book is to demystify risk analysis in construction. The text is
intended to be a concise, practical introduction to systematic
methods of dealing with risk in construction projects. There is
enough material to equip the reader to carry out competent and
thorough analyses of project risk. The book is intended to be a
practical source of reference on the **techniques** of risk analysis used
in construction economics and project management. Mathematics,
jargon and excessive theoretical detail are all avoided, as far as
possible. No prior knowledge of mathematics is assumed (Chapter
2 contains a very simple introduction to some basic notions of
probability). The focus of the book is on the **analysis** rather than
the **management** of risk. At the core of the book several techniques
are introduced. Their strengths and weaknesses are examined to
see how they may be used in practice to carry out risk appraisals
of various aspects of construction projects and capital investment
decisions. Certain techniques are necessary, but not sufficient, for
competent risk analysis. Projects are managed by people. People
enter data, assumptions and judgements into equations for the
purpose of analysis. People's assumptions and perceptions may be
inaccurate and inconsistent, but are often powerfully accurate and
consistent.

This book does not encourage a mechanistic approach. It sets
out to encourage independent thought and maturity of judgement
about projects. The worked examples cover building, civil
engineering and infrastructure work and illustrate how risks may
be dealt with by construction clients (and their consultants) and
contractors.

Many books and papers on the economics of construction,

estimating and forecasting contain ritual declarations of the 'uniqueness' of construction:

- Each project is different.
- There are special problems in construction.
- The future cannot be forecast.
- Construction is a high-risk business.

These pleas are sometimes accompanied by suggestions that, in construction, 'different' rules (covering payment and service delivery) should apply. Personally, I do not agree with most of this. Of course, many industries have their own special characteristics, but few are so special that they cannot be understood by an outsider. Viewing the industry in this way (in terms of its special difficulties) seems to be rather negative and unhelpful. In fact, viewed systematically, there are many features common to a wide range of construction projects. Most projects will have a start date and a finish date. Most projects will be designed and built by teams of people and firms drawn together for that particular project. Most projects will have a design and a construction phase which may, or may not, overlap. Most projects will require contractors to marshal labour, equipment, materials and components to a specific site. Many physical elements of construction will recur across projects. For example, all bridges need a deck and a supporting structure. All buildings need substructures, cladding and services. Although each project may appear to be physically different, construction projects in general exhibit lower levels of complex technical innovation when compared, say, with aerospace, defence or computer software projects.

Of course, the specific details, specification and precise measurements of each project are unique. Plans, estimates and time schedules have to be made in advance with limited information. Judgements about the future have to be made and built in to plans and forecasts. However, focusing on risk in this way may lead to negative attitudes and to the desire not to embark on the project at all in order to avoid all the possible unpleasant consequences. Excessive concern with the negative aspects of risks may lead to overcautious and irrational decisions. In construction, as in life in general, it is necessary to strike a balance between rigid adherence to the status quo, avoiding all risks on the one hand, and rash risk-seeking behaviour on the other. The growth and development of a business, an economy or an individual, require the exercise of judgement and the taking of decisions involving some uncertainty of outcome. To avoid all risks is to stagnate and ultimately to be overtaken by events and die. In business in general, and in construction projects in particular, the question is not whether to take risks but how to take reasonable risks. Our task is not to avoid risk but to recognize it, assess it and manage it.

Risk analysis needs to be carried out in the context of a systematic approach to the management of risk. The point of the analysis is to establish the extent of risk in order to do something about it. The primary focus of these chapters is on the analysis, not the management, of risk. However, neither can be examined in isolation. The purpose of this chapter is therefore to introduce some basic notions of risk, risk analysis and risk management.

1.2 RISK AND UNCERTAINTY: DEFINITIONS

The future is largely unknown. Most business decision making takes place on the basis of **expectations** about the future. Making a decision on the basis of assumptions, expectations, estimates and forecasts of future events involves taking risks. Risk is an abstract concept. It is difficult to define and, in most cases, impossible to measure with any precision. In the context of the management and economics of construction projects, a working definition of risk and uncertainty would be along the following lines:

Risk and uncertainty characterize situations where the **actual** outcome for a particular event or activity is likely to deviate from the estimate or forecast value.

Risk can travel in two directions: the outcome may be better or worse than originally expected. These are known as **upside** and **downside** risks. Risk and uncertainty will apply to the forecast price or time for the entire project and for any subcomponent, subcontract, operation or activity within it. Similarly, risk and uncertainty will be attached to assumptions about weather, inflation, strikes and other external aspects of projects. Taking these latter points into account, risk has also been defined as:

> Exposure to the possibility of economic and financial loss or gain, physical damage or injury, or delay as a consequence of the uncertainty associated with pursuing a particular course of action (Chapman, 1991).

Some people like to distinguish between **risk** and **uncertainty**. The distinction is usually that risk is taken to have quantifiable attributes, whereas uncertainty does not. Risk analysis and risk management had their origins in the insurance industry in the USA in the 1940s. Hence, a **risk** arose when it was possible to make a statistical assessment of the probability of occurrence of a particular event. Risks, therefore, tended to be **insurable**. Using this logic, the actual risk to be carried was quantified as follows:

Risk = Probability of event × Magnitude of loss/gain

Uncertainty, on the other hand, was used to describe situations where it was not possible to attach a probability to the likelihood of occurrence of an event. Uncertainties tended not to be insurable. It is not possible, actuarially, to assess the level of premium required to cover something which is classed as an **uncertainty**. There is much doubt about the practical usefulness of this distinction, especially as the vast majority of business decisions are made without the benefit of statistical data and statistical calculations. Most business decisions are made on subjective judgements, sometimes backed up by appropriate quantitative analysis. The distinction does, however, have some conceptual value. After all, **uncertainty** attached to a high impact event represents a **greater unknown** than a quantified risk attached to the same event. However, the unknown may be shown to have been either more or less likely than the known risk. For the practical purposes of decision making in project management this distinction serves little useful purpose.

Let us explore this briefly with some practical, project-related examples.

Given that we know, from meteorological data gathered over a period of years, the mean and standard deviation of the rainfall in, let us say, Moscow, in October, we can quantify, within measurable confidence limits, the probability that there will be more than five centimetres of rain next October with consequent effects on the water table for a specific site near Red Square. Thus, it is possible to calculate the probability that sheet-piling will be necessary. With this information we can proceed to make a risk-adjusted decision on whether to allow for this in a cost or time forecast. Uncertainty, on the other hand, is assumed in that approach to be not quantifiable. For example, consider the long-term planning for a major project such as a new, privately financed, rapid transport system. The viability of the project depends, among other things, on whether the excess of ticket revenue over capital, running and finance costs is sufficient to give a reasonable return given the very large risks involved. This particular model will need to be built *ex ante*, that is pre-design, pre-site acquisition, pre-statutory permission. The level of ticket revenue will be a function of the number of passengers carried, the price of the ticket and the extent, if any, of government subsidy to take account of other beneficial spillover effects such as reduction of congestion. The number of passengers carried will be a function of, among other things, the economic conditions prevailing at the time and the cost and relative convenience of other forms of transport. Unlike the case of the meteorological records above, there will be no organized statistical database for most of these variables. Yet, in the classic definition of risk, it is likely that the **actual** will deviate from the **expected**. Those who differentiate would regard these variables as **uncertain**. While not exactly non-quantifiable, the latter group is certainly considerably **less** quantifiable than the expected rainfall of the earlier example. Note that in all cases we are concerned with making good decisions before the event, on the basis of limited information. Therefore, we are concerned with **opinions, professional judgements** or **degrees of belief** about the events.

Thus, for those who make the distinction, the only difference between risk and uncertainty is not one of substance, it is one of **degree** (of personal knowledge about the future event). For this reason it seems preferable not to differentiate between risk and uncertainty. No cost estimating, forecasting or project management situation comes to mind where such a distinction would serve

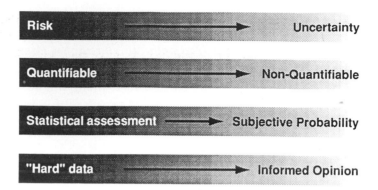

Figure 1.1 The risk–uncertainty continuum

any useful purpose. In this text the terms are used interchangeably. There may be a strong or a weak degree of belief in an event. This degree of belief may be largely, or not at all, quantifiable. There will nearly always be an **informed** opinion of some kind about the variable in question.

Risk and uncertainty may, therefore, be viewed as at either end of the continuum. This is illustrated schematically in Figure 1.1. Risk is at the more assessable end of the continuum: there may even be some statistical data from which to produce an evaluation of the likelihood and size of the potential risk. Uncertainty is at the less assessable end: there will be no 'data'; the decision maker will need to rely on informed opinion. It is possible, though, to attach, loosely, some numbers to subjective opinions. As long as the numbers are a fair representation of that person's opinion, they are useful. A well-informed decision is one which makes use of all available relevant information, both objective and subjective.

1.3   RISK EXPOSURE AND RISK ATTITUDE

Few, if any, business decisions are statistically repeatable. Few have full statistical support in the form of detailed historical data relevant to the current decision. Most decisions of this type are matters of judgement, sometimes supported by data. Risk analysis attempts to enhance the value of these judgements by enabling decision makers to make use of the full extent of their knowledge and experience through formal consideration of risk and uncertainty.

✗For most business decisions there are four main categories of risk, as follows:

> High probability–high impact
> Low probability–high impact
> High probability–low impact
> Low probability–low impact   ✗

The impacts may be positive or negative, upside or downside. The least important type of risk is the low probability–low impact risk. However, even this type of risk needs to be assessed in order to determine whether it has the potential to push non-critical operations into the critical path. Hence, in a formal risk analysis all risks should be considered at the outset. It is quite possible that after an initial analysis the low impact risks of both low and high probability may be eliminated as inconsequential. Using one of the definitions given above, the **exposure** to risk would be given by the probability of the event multiplied by the extent of the potential loss/gain.

It is commonly perceived that economic progress cannot take place without the taking of risks. People are frequently categorized as risk neutral, risk seeking or risk averse. Successful business people are perceived as risk seekers. Risk has about it an aura of achievement. Those who have successfully dealt with risky situations are held in high regard. These assumptions are contradicted by scientific studies of the attitudes of business people. Empirical studies have shown that it is often the case that business decision makers are highly risk averse. In fact they spend a lot of time and effort minimizing the risks that they do take. Similarly, professional gamblers are regarded as risk takers. In fact, successful professional gamblers are also very risk averse. They spend large amounts of effort calculating and minimizing their risk. Attitudes to risk are discussed in detail in Chapter 4.

1.4 RISK IN PROJECTS

1.4.1 Project heterogeneity

The construction industry generally has a bad reputation for its work. The industry has a reputation for time and cost overruns. This may be summed up in the commonly held perception that the industry tends to deliver expensive buildings late. Examples may be quoted from many countries. Is this reputation deserved? This section examines the environment and conditions for cost, price and time forecasting and project management in the context of the construction industry.

Most building and many civil engineering projects consist of a similar set of construction activities involving a variety of materials and specifications on different sites. Most completed buildings

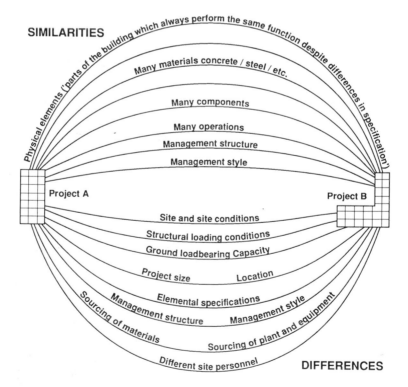

Figure 1.2 Project heterogeneity

have the same set of elements such as substructure, frame, external walls, internal partitions, services and a roof. The result of this is that while it is a cliché and an overstatement to say that every project is unique, it is true that there are large differences between projects. Despite largely common activities and processes, each project is assembled and constructed on its own site with its own physical characteristics, subject to weather conditions depending on the season, with different material specifications and technical solutions to the problems of enclosing space. While a number of materials and components will be identical, many will not. Each project usually has a different labour force of operatives and managers. Hence, there will be differences in the management and interpersonal behaviour on each project simply because people are different. Similar arguments apply to civil engineering and infrastructure projects except that they are usually less homogeneous than building projects.

1.4.2   Budgeting and tender price forecasting

During the design process the client endeavours – usually with the assistance of professional advisers who may be in-house or external – to set a budget, to predict the tender price and to manage the design so that it meets budget. In forecasting the tender price the client's advisers are attempting to forecast the winning tender.

The winning tender will consist of an estimate of the contractor's costs and a mark-up. It is reasonable to expect that the mark-up will usually represent a smaller proportion of the total bid than the cost estimate. Hence, the tender price forecast is, largely, a forecast of the contractor's forecast of what the project is likely to cost. In other words, a forecast of a forecast. This is illustrated in Figure 1.3.

It is often said that during the bidding process the contractor is attempting to assess the correct market price for a project not yet built, to a design which is subject to revision, on a site about which there is little information and with a labour force not yet recruited.

Construction people sometimes suggest that under these conditions it is surprising that it is possible to produce a price at all. While that may be something of an overstatement it does seem

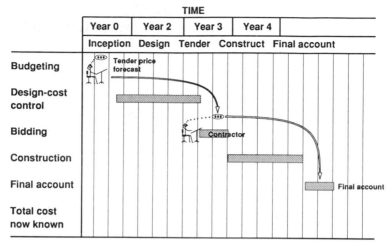

Figure 1.3 A forecast of a forecast

reasonable to suggest that such problems as these are infinitely (now there **is** an overstatement) more difficult at the earlier budget stage. The task of the client's quantity surveyor, for example, is to forecast the contractor's forecast without access to the contractor's data and with many more inherent uncertainties caused by not yet having a design or, perhaps, even a site. The budget decision is made at a much earlier point in the life of the project and so the forecast is being made over a much longer timescale.

In addition to all of this there is some dispute about what is actually being forecast. Is it the lowest tender? What if the lowest tender is a mistake? Perhaps we are trying to forecast the average of all the tenders received. This average will be influenced by errors made by bidders at the top and bottom end of the range and by cover prices at the top end of the range. Additionally, the actual price for constructing the project will not be known until the project is complete and all accounts have been agreed, if not settled. The range of possible targets is illustrated in Figure 1.4. It is probably safe to assume that, in most cases, the lowest tender is not an error. Where the lowest tender is an error, this will be clear to the quantity surveying team who may recommend further investigation and possibly the acceptance of another tender. Therefore, what we are trying to forecast is the accepted tender. This accepted tender represents the winning contractor's estimate of the

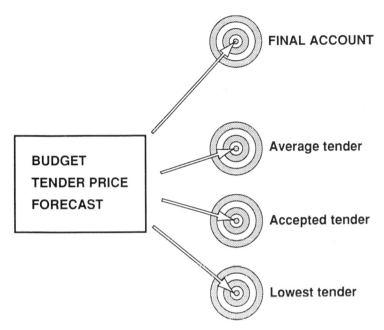

Figure 1.4 Range of available targets for budget forecasts

market price for constructing the project. This estimate may or may not eventually be shown to be a correct estimate of the actual outturn cost of the project to the contractor. Clearly, if the contractor's estimate proves to have been optimistic, then the achieved profit margin will reduce. The converse is also the case. This is too simplistic a view, of course, as it assumes that other things are equal. Specifically, it assumes that there will have been no variations or design changes and that the contractor has taken no control action to reduce costs during the course of the project. The nature of construction is such that no matter how well designed the project, it will usually require some fine adjustments. Some inflation, or perhaps a change of mind on some detail from the client. Changes of this sort can be minimized by appropriate contractual arrangements. But it is unrealistic to expect that the precise details of the project as constructed will be exactly as they were envisaged at the budget or tender stage, except in rare cases. This highlights one of the differences between forecasting and budgeting in construction and business forecasting. Business forecasting is concerned with forecasting phenomena that may subse-

☐ Precise ground conditions of site
☐ Substructure design
☐ Detailed superstructure design
☐ Timing of project
☐ Type of contract arrangements
☐ Inflation (medium term: two to five years)
☐ Construction market conditions (anticipated)

Figure 1.5 Risks and uncertainties affecting construction budgeting decisions

quently be measured, such as sales, inflation and share price. In construction, on the other hand, the forecast is mostly concerned with estimates. Some specific risks and uncertainties affecting construction budgeting decisions are suggested in Figure 1.5.

In budgeting and forecasting for construction projects, as in many other fields, it is sometimes necessary to remember that we have a tendency to believe that the more precise a statement is, the more accurate it is. We are all familiar with the illusion of precision given when the answer to a problem is given on a computer printout to six decimal places. In construction budgeting, judge-

Technical   – Adequacy of site investigation
              – Availability of materials and components
              – Adequacy of design and design
                information
Logistical   – Sourcing materials, plant and labour
Construction – Productivity
              – Weather
              – Adequacy of contractor's own
                construction plan
              – Adequacy of resource scheduling
              – Industrial relations
Financial   – Escalation/inflation (short term)
              – Payment schedule

Figure 1.6 Risks and uncertainties affecting the contractor's estimate

1. Cost of materials — discounts, different suppliers, speed of payment, vertical integration
2. Labour productivity — skill, standard of workmanship
3. Labour costs — wages, overtime, good staff
4. Wastage — materials, labour, theft
5. Plant — amount, type, own/hire
6. Site techniques — different sequence of operations
7. Allowance for fixed price — future increased costs
8. Effect of design team
9. Deliberate distortion — front loading and cash flow, anticipating variations
10. Overheads
11. Profit

Figure 1.7 Same project, different contractor

ments have to be made between being roughly accurate or being precisely wrong.

Moving through time to the point where the majority of the design work is done and tender documentation has been produced, there will still remain many areas where judgements about risk and uncertainty will need to be made by the contractor in order to prepare an estimate. Some of these are illustrated in Figure 1.6.

It follows, then, that there will be good reasons for differences in estimates produced by different contractors for the same project. These are summarized in Figure 1.7.

1.4.3 Project-based sources of risk

For any given project the major sources of risk are: size, complexity, novelty, speed of design and construction and location. There is an abundance of empirical evidence on project cost and time overruns which indicates that initial forecasts are far too optimistic and that project risks are not being dealt with adequately.

Consider a stereotypical project life cycle from inception through to commissioning and operating. At any given point the

☐   Size
☐   Complexity
☐   Novelty
☐   Intensity (speed of design and construction)
☐   Physical location

Figure 1.8 Major sources of project risk

project participants have only expectations about the future. They do not, as it were, **know** what will happen next. They can only work on reasonable assumptions. Sources of project risk are summarized in Figure 1.8.

1.4.4   External risks

Change is an unavoidable feature of all large projects. The world of construction is one where timescales are relatively long, where there is time for variability. The longer the time scale is, the more likely it is that there will be some interference or outside event which affects the project. These are fertile conditions for things to go wrong. All of this together emphasizes the need for forecasts and plans to allow realistically for change. Categories of risk, internal and external, to projects are illustrated in Figure 1.9 and Table 1.1.

☐   Inflation
☐   Market conditions
☐   Cost escalation on input resources
☐   Materials ⎫
    Labour   ⎬ availability
☐   Political uncertainty
☐   Weather

Figure 1.9 Sources of risk external to the project

1.5   AN OVERVIEW OF RISK MANAGEMENT

Most commentators on construction risk start with a consideration of what is known as the **risk management cycle**. This is illustrated

Table 1.1   A list of major categories of sources of risk

SOURCE	EXAMPLE
Client/government/ regulatory agencies	Bureaucratic delays, changes in local regulations
Funding/fiscal	Changes in government funding policy, liaison between several funders
Definition of project	Change in project scope
Project organization	Authority of project manager, involvement of outside bodies
Design	Adequacy to meet need, realism of design programme
Local conditions	Local customs, weather windows
Permanent plant supply	Degree of novelty, damage/loss during transportation
Construction contractors	Experience, financial stability
Construction materials	Excessive wastage, reliability of quality
Construction labour	Industrial relations, multiracial labour force
Construction plant	Resale value, spares availability
Logistics	Remoteness, access to site
Estimating data	Relevance to specific project availability
Inflation	
Exchange rates	
Force majeure	

Source: Hayes et al. (1986), p. 12.

LIVERPOOL JOHN MOORES UNIVERSITY
Aldham Robarts L.R.C.
TEL. 051 231 3701/3634

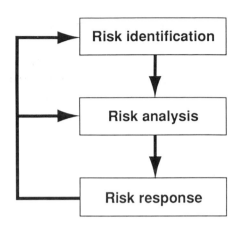

Figure 1.10 Risk management

in Figure 1.10. The cycle is useful insofar as it focuses the mind in a systematic way on the identification, analysis and response to risk. The whole purpose of risk analysis is to help the decision maker to consider a rational response to the degree of exposure to risk which is revealed by the identification and analysis stages.

1.5.1 Risk identification

The risk identification stage has received the least attention in the literature on risk. Many professionals who have accumulated some experience of carrying out risk analysis on capital projects find that the identification stage is the most time consuming. Identification of risks internal and external to the project requires that the analyst be systematic, experienced and creative. It is frequently the case that the best way to gain access to this range of personal qualities is by assembling an appropriate team. It is not realistic to expect 20/20 foresight. Construction professionals are required in law to exercise reasonable care and skill in carrying out their work. The identification of risks is about making the best use of the information and experience available at the time of making the decision. In practice I have found that it is useful to work closely with the project team and to consider explicitly at least three separate areas:

1. Risks internal to the project, by breaking the project down into major work packages.

2. Risks external to the project and emanating from the business and physical environment.

3. Consider the client, the project, the project team and the quality of the documentation from the perspectives of the various contractors in anticipation of sources of claims.

It may be necessary to consider the use of a formal technique for teasing out an exhaustive range of potential problems. Formal brainstorming is sometimes used in this context. A formal brainstorming session should have a set of clear rules and a timetable. A coordinator should be appointed, and it is essential that he or she has two qualities: the ability to chair meetings and a sense of humour. The first stage is the creative session where the coordinator elicits one idea at a time from individuals on potential risks or sources of risk. Individual team members are not restricted to their own knowledge domain. The rule of this stage is that no criticisms of ideas or people are allowed. Outlandish suggestions are encouraged. A list of suggestions is maintained on a flipchart or similar device. As the list contains no names, there is no way of associating any particular idea with any particular member of the team. Stage two of the session is quite different in character; it is the evaluation stage, when all the ideas are evaluated seriously and a final list is made. The list is the product of the team rather than the individual members.

Two other aspects of risk identification are worth mentioning here. First, if the team members are committed to the project and motivated towards achieving a successful outcome overall, then the whole process of risk analysis should be a positive experience. Someone once said (not about risk analysis), 'If it isn't fun then you probably aren't doing it right'. Second, it is sometimes argued that risk analysis encourages negative and cautious attitudes among the team or the project sponsors. If this is happening it needs to be taken seriously and examined closely to ascertain whether it is a realistic assessment of the problems associated with the project. At the same time the analyst needs to maintain some distance from the project in order to avoid 'falling in love' with it. This affliction will be dissected more fully in Chapter 8.

1.5.2   Risk analysis

As the techniques of analysis form the focus of the bulk of these chapters, we shall not dwell upon them here.

1.5.3   Risk response

The purpose of the identification and the analysis is to enable the decision maker to make a considered response **in advance** of the problem occurring. The general guiding principle of risk response is that the parties to the project should seek a collaborative and, insofar as is possible, mutually beneficial distribution of risk. The starting point for the distribution of risk is the contract. A dominant party unthinkingly offloading all the project risks to others is unlikely to enhance the chances of a successful outcome to the project. Responses to identified risk are usually listed as follows: retention, reduction, transfer, avoidance.

A number of factors should be taken into account when allocating risks among parties to the project. First, the best way to avoid all risk is not to proceed with the project. The benefits of the project must be judged to be worth the risks involved in undertaking it. Second, it seems sensible to place the risk under the responsibility of the party who has the best possibility of controlling it. Third, risks should be allocated where possible to the party for whom the risks are least onerous. Fourth, although it is reasonable to exact a premium for carrying a specific project risk, the party responsible should be left with some motivation to avoid and minimize risk consequences should unfortunate events occur.

Responding to anticipated risks by collaborating on the equitable distribution of risk should lead to long-term economies in the industry.

1.6   RISK ANALYSIS: ADVANTAGES AND LIMITATIONS

All forecasts about the future are uncertain. From first principles, it seems entirely unreasonable to disguise this fact in making the forecast. At the same time, decisions have to be made, budgets have to be allocated and development potential maximized. Systematic analysis of risk exposure must, over time, lead to a more efficient allocation of resources. Even without producing quantitative results, the very discipline of breaking a project down into its sources of risk and systematically examining them ensures that the estimator develops a much more realistic feel for the project and its range of possible outcomes.

Virtually all writers and consultants on risk agree that there is no such thing as a software-only solution to the problem of risk management. Risk analysis software is neither **necessary** nor **sufficient** for risk management. Rigorous, comprehensive and competent risk analysis is primarily dependent on the attitude of mind of the appropriate decision makers and their advisers. Risk management will not remove all risks; it will enable explicit decisions to be made which will mitigate the potential effect of certain risks. Risk management will also assist in rational, **defensible** decisions regarding the allocation of risks among the parties to the project. Risk analysis is not a substitute for professional experience and judgement. On the contrary, it helps professionals to make use of the full extent of their experience and knowledge by liberating them from the necessity of making simplifying assumptions in order to produce deterministic plans and forecasts. Risk analysis is a supplement to, not a substitute for, professional judgement.

Fully documented risk studies of project estimates are helpful in subsequently 'defending' estimators' decisions. There is a useful distinction between good **luck** and good **management** (Chapman, 1991). For example, it may subsequently be necessary to defend a budget which had been set high initially in order to take account of a risk which, either through good management or good luck, did not in the event occur. Conversely, it may be necessary to support a subsequent request for additional project resources to cover an outcome which, although originally foreseen, was thought to be highly unlikely. Thus, one of the many uses of this form of analysis is in distinguishing bad **luck** from **bad management** and, of course, **good luck** from **good management**. Thus, in subsequent project *post mortems* it is possible to distinguish controllable from uncontrollable events. For a budget estimate, full documentation of the risk analysis need not necessarily be more than a few sides of A4 paper. According to Chapman (1991) documentation is important in another respect: in situations where experienced professional staff move on to different posts, good documentation ensures that the firm will retain its 'corporate' knowledge of the risk analysis and also facilitate the induction of new staff.

Probabilistic forecasts increase the quality of information available to senior managers who have to take decisions about which projects shall receive funding. They also render it possible to consider contingencies, across portfolios of projects, in a meaningful way. There should be no doubt that the implementation of risk management procedures will lead, over time, to a more efficient use of resources.

In summary, many writers, consultants and users of risk management agree on the following benefits from the approach:

- There is an overall reduction in risk exposure;
- Pre-planning should lead to the use of pre-evaluated and prompt responses to any risks which do materialize;
- More explicit decision making on the project;
- Clearer definition of specific risks associated with particular projects;
- Full use is made of the skill and experience of project personnel;
- Good documentation ensures that corporate knowledge of project risks accumulates over time and does not remain with individuals;
- Situations where there is little, no or unreliable data are not ones where it is not possible to carry out the analysis, they are situations where the analysis is **more**, not less, important.

1.7   SUMMARY

This chapter is an introduction to the basic ideas of risk analysis and risk management and their application in the planning and appraisal of construction projects. The terms risk and uncertainty are clarified at the outset and a conceptual framework is presented which separates risk exposure from risk attitude. The specific problems of budgeting and tender price forecasting are then considered. Sources of risk both internal and external to the project are identified. An overview of the process of risk management then forms the background for the introduction of a number of techniques of risk analysis. The chapter concludes by considering the limitations and the advantages of risk analysis and risk management.

CHAPTER 2

UNDERSTANDING PROBABILITIES

2.1 INTRODUCTION

This book is concerned with risk analysis and individual and corporate attitudes to risk. It sets out a clear framework for dealing with quantitative and qualitative aspects of risk analysis. This includes both entering considered judgements to the analysis and interpreting the eventual output of the process. It is possible to deal with risk competently, consistently, and comprehensively with the use of very little mathematics. An understanding of the rudiments of probability and of utility theory nevertheless adds considerably to the focus of the professional who needs to make decisions under conditions of risk and uncertainty.

2.2 PROBABILITY

A probability is a number, between zero and one inclusive, which represents a judgement about the perceived relative likelihood of some event. Zero implies the event is impossible, one implies that it is certain. This number obeys several mathematical laws, most of which derive from the basic rule that the sum of probabilities of a set of mutually exclusive events, one of which must happen, is 1. This judgement may be derived from one or a combination of three sources (Figure 2.1).

First, it may be an 'objective' calculation based on observed relative frequencies of past incidences of the same event; for example, the number of times when there has been more than two inches of rainfall in November in central London. This type of judgement only applies to identical **repeatable** events.

A commonly quoted example is the tossing of a coin. Using a strictly 'scientific and objective', so-called frequentist, approach we would be left with figures such as 535/1000 or 11 004/20 000. These figures, while not actually probabilities themselves, are known as **unbiased estimators**, which means they are good, but fallible, guesses of that probability. Notice that two people each running a set of experiments could quite easily arrive at different answers. It is the method of arriving at the probability which is 'objective', not the figure itself. The probability itself would be defined under this approach as the limit which the ratio of heads to tails reaches as the number of tosses tends to infinity. For this frequentist approach the event must be repeatable under substantially similar conditions. Therefore this method is unsuitable for most real-world problems.

Second, there may be some a priori basis, derived from some visible symmetry, for a particular probability. This renders unnecessary the collection of frequency observations. For a perfectly balanced coin the probability of flipping a head is 0.5, if we assume away the small chance that the coin may land on its edge. Similarly, for a perfectly balanced die, the probability of throwing a six, or any specific number between one and six, is 1/6. This second approach gives intuitively correct clear numbers.

The third possibility for deriving a probability is the so-called personalistic view or subjective probability. This is a reflection of consistent opinions and judgements about an event. People frequently make verbal statements about probabilities and choices about gambles. These opinions and choices reflect the subject's own degree of belief in the relative likelihood of an event. In the absence of an a priori basis for judgement the personalistic view allows just as meaningful a discussion of unique events as of repeatable events – if any event which is not an experiment can appropriately be called repeatable. Thus, subjective probability offers the only way to deal with many of the problems encountered in real-world decisions where the event in question is unlikely to

☐   Objective probabilities
  –   based on observed relative frequencies
      of past incidences of the same event
  –   applies to repeatable events only
☐   A priori probabilities
  –   derived from a visible symmetry
  –   the coin / dice
☐   Subjective probabilities
  –   a reflection of consistent opinions and judgements about an event
  –   a reflection of the subject's own degree of belief in the
      likelihood of an event
  –   applies to any event

Figure 2.1 Three types of probability

be repeated and may often be unique. For example, how likely is it that interest rates will fall over the next year? How likely is it that inflation will remain below 5% in the next year?

There has been much controversy in statistics revolving around a distrust of personalistic probabilities by the frequentists. In many textbooks on statistics, probabilities refer to an **event** while in texts on decision analysis and operational research, probability may refer to an **opinion** about an event. In most real-world situations there is no possibility of repeating events under substantially identical conditions. Similarly, there is often little possibility of gathering large sets of relative frequency data. Thus, for most practical purposes, and certainly in the majority of problems in building economics, we shall be dealing with personal probabilities. Probabilities in general are often quite difficult to deal with in cost models because, with the exception of probabilities of zero and one, it is impossible to prove them right or wrong. Personal subjective probabilities are even more difficult due to psychological factors. Namely, there is significant (although disputed) evidence to show that people make systematic errors in deriving subjective probabilities. These errors and biases are discussed in more detail in Chapter 3.

2.3   PERSONAL PROBABILITIES

There are two approaches to the eliciting of subjective probabilities: the direct and indirect methods. The direct method assumes the existence of a rational decision maker well aware of the rudiments of probability and consists merely of asking the subject to assign a number to his or her opinion about the outcome in question. The indirect method consists of asking a series of questions, from the answers to which it is possible to impute the personal probability. Such questioning follows along the lines of utility theory, which is discussed in Chapter 4. It is assumed here that construction professionals will be sufficiently aware of the probability calculus to enable the direct method to be used.

Luckily for the elicitors of probabilities, they can never be proved wrong in probability assessments other than zero and one.

The empirical literature on decision science is now quite well developed and it is possible to derive a number of practical suggestions for the eliciting of personal probabilities. In the interests of crisp advice we shall need to make some fairly general statements.

In general, people have a tendency to overestimate low probabilities. Specifically, an expert would prefer to warn of some possible, though unlikely, dire outcome and be proved wrong than to have not predicted it at all. Hence, it is good practice never to ask about the probability of a specific event without also asking about the probability of its complement or complements. It is good practice to ask the same question a number of different ways in a search for inconsistencies in the answers. If you find inconsistencies, be happy. They may be very beneficial as they can be given as feedback to the subject and form the basis of more detailed consideration of the problem. It has been shown that experts have a tendency to be overconfident in their judgements. For example in a large number of studies people were asked to answer questions and then to assess the probability that they had given the correct answers. It was found that while there **is** a correlation between people's subjective confidence and their objective accuracy, they are not well **calibrated**. For example, individuals who were 85% confident in their answers may in fact have got 75% correct. The generalized finding is that experts **do** make better judgements but their **metacognition** (self-knowledge) is poor. Thus, when eliciting a probability for a specific event it is good practice to spend some time considering why that judgement may turn out to be wrong. It seems to be nearly always preferable to use a group of experts rather than individuals. Each expert will have slightly different perspectives to contribute and the whole is likely to be more than the sum of the parts. However, there is evidence to suggest that personal interaction between the experts should be avoided. For this reason the use of the so-called Delphi methods is suggested in Chapter 5. Delphi methods enable a group of experts to have access to each other's ideas without personal interaction. This helps to avoid bias derived from the overconfidence of particular individuals and from the effect of personalities, as opposed to technical skills, on the work of the group.

2.4 JOINT AND COMPOUND PROBABILITY

The 'laws' of probability enable calculations on joint and compound probabilities as follows. The probability of one or a number of mutually exclusive outcomes is calculated by **adding** together the probabilities of the individual events. This is known as the joint probability of the set of outcomes. For example, if I place bets on two horses in the same six-horse race, then the probability of my winning is calculated by adding together the probabilities of both individual horses. Unrealistically assuming that each horse has an equal chance of winning, then my probability of winning would be given by

$$1/6 + 1/6 = 0.33.$$

On the other hand, if I place a so-called accumulator bet, where I place bets on horses in two separate races such that if the first horse wins then the winnings are placed on the horse in the second race, then the probability of my winning overall would be given by the product of the probabilities of each horse winning its own race. Thus, for the purpose of discussion, using the same simplifying but unrealistic assumption as above, the probability of winning would be given by the following expression:

$$1/6 \times 1/6 = 0.027.$$

The figure of 0.027 speaks for itself as a deterent against placing accumulator bets. This is a **compound** probability where we are interested in calculating the overall likelihood of a number of independent events occurring together. This has a well-known application in the construction field. Consider the budget forecast for a new library to serve a rapidly expanding neighbourhood. This is summarized in Table 2.1. The budget has been broken down into four major headings. Each is given a best (most likely) estimate and a worst case. The decision rule for deriving the worst case estimate is that it should represent an event which would not occur more often than one time in ten. Let us, therefore, assign a notional probability of 0.1 for each worst case. Assuming that the figures have been correctly estimated and that the components of the budget are independent of each other, then the probability of the

Table 2.1   Budget forecast for new library

BUDGET COMPONENT	MOST LIKELY		WORST CASE (P=0.1)	
Site purchase	£500 000		£600 000	
Substructure	£250 000		£310 000	
Superstructure	£750 000		£950 000	
Sub-total		£1 500 000		£1 860 000
Escalation	10%	£150 000	15%	£279 000
Totals		£1 650 000		£2 139 000

project costing £2 139 000 is given as follows:

$$0.1 \times 0.1 \times 0.1 \times 0.1 = 0.0001$$

The example is simplistic but it does illustrate that in considering the probability of a number of worst cases happening together, the odds rapidly diminish to very small numbers indeed – in this case, 1000 to one.

2.5   EXPECTED MONETARY VALUE

Similarly, probability may be used to calculate the expected outcome of a decision which has a range of probabilities and contingent outcomes. Consider the simple example of a lottery ticket which gives the owner a 0.75 chance of winning £5000 with a complementary 0.25 chance of winning nothing. The expected monetary value (EMV) of the ticket is given as follows:

$$\text{EMV} = 0.75 \times £5000 + 0.25 \times £0$$

$$= £3750$$

This implies that if, over a large number of transactions, I can purchase these tickets for less than £3750 than I shall gain. If I purchase the tickets at a higher price then I shall inevitably lose over time. If I buy them at exactly £3750, then over time I shall neither win nor lose. The EMV should realistically be viewed only in the context of a large number of identical transactions. Unfortunately it is sometimes used inappropriately to assess decisions of a more unique nature.

2.6 SUMMARY

In this chapter we have introduced some very basic ideas of probability, specifically aimed at those with no previous exposure to the subject. We saw that there were three possible probabilities: objective, intuitively obvious and subjective. In real-world situations, such as those faced in construction projects every day, we normally only deal with professional judgement or subjective probability. Some practical aspects of eliciting personal probabilities were discussed. Simple calculations of joint and compound probability and expected monetary value were demonstrated.

CHAPTER 3

FORECASTING: PSYCHOLOGICAL ASPECTS

3.1 INTRODUCTION

This chapter sets out to help estimators to view their work more systematically and to make allowances for common human errors of judgement. When we refer to **estimators** or **forecasters** we are referring to those quantity surveyors, architects, engineers or other professionals working for consultants, developers, clients and contractors in the process of budgeting and carrying out design cost control and the management of construction projects.

How and why do errors and biases creep into estimates and forecasts? Are there patterns of bias? Is it possible for a trained professional to anticipate and pre-emptively to adjust for certain types of predictable bias? This chapter is concerned with exploring and answering those questions. Two sources of bias are identified: people's own inherent errors and biases; and the biases which are introduced when people talk to or report to each other, especially when the reporting is up and down a managerial or power hierarchy. Patterns may be identified in both types of bias. We preface the material on biases with a brief consideration of the nature of rules of thumb.

3.2 RULES OF THUMB

It is known that people use rules of thumb (sometimes called heuristics) in decision making. This is a rational response to dealing with a complicated world. The most time-consuming and sometimes the most difficult part of decision making is frequently the gathering in and analysis of data relevant to the problem in hand. This may be exemplified by the common problem of exploring two outline design alternatives. Much time is spent in clarifying specifications and perhaps in roughly measuring and pricing approximate quantities. The actual making of the decision, the moment of choice, where the client, through his or her advisers, decides to choose the lowest cost or the shortest time or the greatest difference between value and cost, may take only a matter of seconds.

The 80/20 rule is commonly used in situations like the one just described. This implies that 80% of the cost of the project may be accounted for by measuring the largest 20% of the units of finished work. It is important to remember that rules of thumb are just that. They are usually anecdotal and should not be followed precisely. Whether 80% of the cost of a project is covered by 20% of the items measured in the bill of quantities depends on which method of measurement was used, who did the measuring and who did the pricing. Clearly, it is highly unlikely that the ratio is exactly 80/20, and it is even more unlikely that the same ratio would crop up from project to project given all of the other differences between projects and contractors. What is true is to suggest that:

> there will be a propensity for a large proportion of the cost of any given project to be accounted for by a relatively small number of expensive items. Consequently, on many construction projects there will also be a large number of relatively cost insignificant items.

This, unfortunately, does not trip off the tongue as easily as '80/20'.

Rules of thumb, such as the 80/20, are usually based on previous experience. This means that they are often close to the personal experience of professionals making judgements and decisions. Unfortunately, it also means that they have a tendency to be backward looking. If underlying conditions change then the rule may no longer be appropriate. For example, the 80/20 rule may be distorted by two factors, which are a continuing feature of the construction industry. First, the ratio will be influenced by the approach taken to the method of measurement. Has the bill been prepared by measuring units of finished work in place, or by measuring operations and taking time- and method-related charges as separate items? Secondly, the ratio will be influenced by changes in the technology of construction. The spread of costs over construction projects will be likely to change as there are changes in the design and in construction methods. The implications are that rules of thumb need to be kept under continuous review to ensure their continuing relevance.

3.3   PERSONAL BIASES

There are two common measures of estimating accuracy. These are **bias** (the mean error) and **consistency** (the range of errors from the mean). There is a very large and complex psychological literature on the subject of judgemental bias. Much of this work had its origin in research in logistics and decision analysis on behalf of the military. Although some of the work is disputed – mostly for being carried out in laboratory settings rather than in the real world – there is a large body of agreement on the existence of three rules of thumb. These are: representativeness, availability, and anchoring and adjustment.

The representativeness heuristic is the process of evaluating the probability of an uncertain event, or a sample, by the degree to which it (i) is similar in essential properties to its parent population, and (ii) reflects the salient features of the process by which it is generated. It is, in essence, an assessment of the degree of correspondence between a sample and a population, an instance and a category, an act and an actor or, more generally, between an outcome and a model. Since information is commonly stored and processed in relation to some mental model of the problem, it is natural and economical for the probability of an event to be evaluated by the degree to which that event is representative of the appropriate mental model. The representativeness heuristic leads to fallacies about base rates and sample size.

The base rate fallacy refers to people's tendency to ignore base rates in favour of, say, individuating information, indicant or diagnostic information, when such is available, rather than to integrate them all. For example, in Question 1, below, the base rate is 0.25. The fact that the last three contracts were completed on time is indicant or diagnostic information. The sample size fallacy is related to the law of large numbers. This states that as the sample size increases, the sample mean tends to be closer and closer to the population mean, and that as the sample size becomes bigger the variance decreases. Therefore, the mean calculated from a large sample tends to be more stable than that from a small sample and the sample variance is comparatively smaller from a larger sample than from a small one. Neglecting this law of large numbers is said to be committing the sample size fallacy in subjective judgements. As neither of these points is easy to understand in the abstract, we shall present two examples.

Consider the following two questions which highlight the base rate fallacy and the sample size fallacy respectively.

---

1.   *Given the history of subcontractor A: 25% of all projects completed on time. You have examined the last three contracts performed by this contractor and all have been completed on time. What is the chance that the forthcoming project, if awarded to contractor A, will be completed on time?*

> A. *50%*
> B. *25%*
> C. *75%*

The 'base rate' suggests that B is the correct answer to this question, i.e. there is a 0.25 likelihood that the contract will be completed on time. To 'commit the base rate fallacy' (a heinous crime to rational decision makers) would be to ignore the base rate in this instance, in favour of the diagnostic information derived from the last three projects. It has been shown over a large number of experiments that lay people will tend to do just that and return an answer like A or C; in other words, they will assume that on the basis of the last three contracts, the contractor's record of completion on time seems to have improved. The psychologists who did the work take the view that this is a 'fallacy', i.e. that people are interpreting the information incorrectly. They say, in effect in this case, that three readings are not enough to negate the base rate. Of course, the question posed in the example is rather simplistic. Real-world problems are hardly, if ever, that clear cut. Now, we are interested here in real-world problems and in the practical application of these ideas. Therefore we had better examine the assumptions which the psychologists had to make in order to establish the notion of a base rate 'fallacy'.

First, they make the assumption that the number of readings available to form the basis of the base rate was large in comparison to the number of readings in the diagnostic information. Thus, statistically in this case, three readings is not enough to warrant a change in the base rate. The second assumption is the one beloved of all economists, namely, 'that other things are equal'. In this case, the assumption is that nothing has changed in the contractor's behaviour. The contractor has taken no controlling action to improve the rate of on-time completions. The project managers have not been sacked or reprimanded. The company has not introduced an incentive scheme to encourage completion on time. One is forced to wonder how such a contractor could remain in business long enough to provide the large number of projects necessary to calculate the base rate.

Even though the assumptions seem rather tight in the case of our example, the concept of the base rate fallacy is useful. It forces the decision maker to ask fundamental questions about whether any underlying conditions have changed before making any forecast on judgement. More importantly, it forces the decision maker to consider the notion of a 'base rate' and new 'diagnostic' information and to question whether the diagnostic information makes a sufficiently strong case for adjusting the longer term trend, or the base rate.

---

2. *A certain town is served by two hospitals. In the larger hospital about 45 babies are born each day, and in the smaller hospital about 15 babies are born each day. As you know, about 50% of all babies are boys. The exact percentage of baby boys, however, varies from day to day. Sometimes it may be higher than 50%, sometimes lower.*

   For a period of 1 year, each hospital recorded the days on which more than 60% of the babies born were boys. Which hospital do you think recorded more such days?

   A. *The larger hospital*
   B. *The smaller hospital*
   C. *About the same*

To repeat, the law of large numbers states that the mean calculated from a sample will become closer to the underlying population mean as the sample gets larger. Means calculated from small samples are less stable than those based on large samples. Logically, therefore, the correct answer is B. Namely, the smaller hospital will supply the greater number of 'variant' readings where more than 60% of the babies born are boys. However, over a large number of experiments significant numbers of lay people, when asked a question along these lines, will supply an answer based on A or C in our example. Effectively, they are neglecting the law of large numbers.

'Availability' is a heuristic which makes use of retrievability of instances. Some event with which one has had personal contact looms more likely than it would statistically. For example, if one of us has had personal contact with an aeroplane accident, a relatively rare event, then we are highly likely to overestimate the likelihood of future similar mishaps.

The following question tests for the use of the availability heuristic.

You are an estimator employed by ACME Contractors Ltd. You are asked to prepare a lump sum estimate for the pile caps [a drawing was attached]. This estimate is to be used to compare the tender submissions of several subcontractors. This pile cap is to be let as a separate subcontract to one of the subcontractors.

The control group did not receive the following paragraph.

You have checked a previous BQ of your company and found the following information:

1. *Reinforced concrete grade 25 N/mm^2 filled into formwork*
   £30.00/m^3
2. *High tensile reinforcement bars cut, bent and bundled*
   16–32 mm diameter *£350.00/tonne*
3. *Formwork to foundation and beds height $> 1\,m$* *£20.00/m^2*
Bear in mind that, due to your company's pricing, these rates are not necessarily the true costs of the respective items.

This question was issued to two groups of student quantity surveyors. The control group did not receive the second paragraph, the data in which was set up to be deliberately well below market rates. A statistically significant difference was found between the answers of the two groups. This implies that the experimental group did make use of this heuristic.

'Adjustment' refers to the cases when people make estimates by starting from an initial value and adjusting it to yield the final answer. Adjustment from an anchor is usually employed in numerical prediction when a relevant value is available. The initial value may be suggested by the formulation of the problem, or it may be the result of a partial computation. Adjustments are typically insufficient in both cases. Anchoring refers to the phenomenon whereby final results are usually biased towards the initial values. Anchoring occurs not only when the starting point is given, but also when the assessor has to base his or her estimate on the result of incomplete computation.

For example, consider the following question which was issued as part of the experiment described earlier. The control group did not receive the second paragraph. No statistical difference could be found between the answers to the two groups, which implies that the estimates were not significantly influenced by the anchor.

A client approaches you and wants to build a new supermarket in Dartford Town Centre. Prepare an estimate for the construction costs for this proposed supermarket, with a gross floor area 10 000 m², 100 parking spaces and associated works.

The control group did not receive the following sentence.

The client has heard reports that a recently finished supermarket for one of his competitors cost £1.5 million.

Psychologists hold that the biases and fallacies resulting from the three heuristics above lead to 'systematic and predictable' errors in judgement. Recent experimental work at the University of Greenwich was only able to find clear evidence to partly support this. Final year, full- and part-time undergraduate students taking courses in building economics were set a number of estimating tasks which had rogue information attached, designed to trip up the subjects and cause them to use the heuristics described. In only one case did they succumb to statistically significant error. This was in using the availability heuristic on the pile cap question and failing to spot that some rates supplied from a recent project had been set well below a reasonable market level.

3.4   REPORTING BIASES

Although subjects such as risk analysis and utility theory have been taught in business schools for more than a quarter of a century, they have only become embedded in building economics syllabuses in the past decade. Traditionally, in construction and property development, estimates and forecasts of, for example, time, costs, prices, rents and returns have been given as single points. There are, sometimes, very good reasons for this. Single-point figures are often needed as 'budgets' for the purposes of planning and control. Some projects need to be managed in such a manner that they are completed by a specified date: for example, exhibition buildings or, say, a harbour to facilitate materials imports for some large and vital infrastructure project. Other projects need to be arranged – even to the extent of downsizing, redesigning or reducing specification – such that the outturn cost is equal to or less than the allowed budget as there may be no possibility of further resources. In such cases single-point figures are indeed necessary as targets for the purposes of day-to-day planning and control. Nevertheless, it remains the case that these single points are **forecasts** and targets, not **certainties**. For most purposes single-point forecasts conceal more than they reveal. Thus, there are fertile conditions for error when an estimate/forecast is produced by an expert or consultant and is then reported to a director, partner or some other senior decision maker. All that said, two important sources of bias in single-point forecasts will be explored here: first, the bias that results from conflict between, on the one hand, the need for better forecasts and, on the other, the method of managerial control using rewards and punishments for over- and underestimation; second the bias and misinterpretation which result from the differences in personal risk attitudes. These sources of bias have been long understood in business schools. Let us explore them in turn. The approach here is an adaptation to construction of work reported in the *Harvard Business Review*.

3.4.1 Conflicting use of forecasts

In many organizations there are reporting systems which involve managers reporting back, with explanations, when projects exceed budgets, or when returns fail to meet the initial target by some arbitrary figure, in many cases 10%. Where a project comes in under budget, or when returns exceed forecasts by more than the same amount, the explanations, although necessary, are not examined in quite the same detail. There are not the same negative implications for the personnel who produced the model or the forecast. When an organization applies negative sanctions to managers who exceed budgets and, say, takes no action of praise or reward when projects come in on or under budget, then there will be a natural tendency to overestimate forecasts of project costs and to underestimate forecasts of project returns or rental. In this case, the figure that gets reported is not necessarily the **most likely**, it may be a very **conservative** figure, i.e. for project costs rather high, and for project returns a rather low figure which is quite likely to be exceeded (Figure 3.1). In either case, this type of reporting will lead, over time, to a misallocation of resources. Many projects which have reasonable likelihoods of achieving healthy returns will not get support as they do not contain a sufficient buffer to ensure the safety of the forecaster in the short term.

Many projects which have a better than even chance of being completed on or under budget will not get support because they cannot be estimated safely enough to protect the forecaster from recrimination in the short term. Let us assume that there are a large number of projects of similar size and profitability which generate similar levels of absolute profit, i.e. no one project exerts excessive influence on the firm or practice. Then it is sufficient for 6 in 10 of the projects to come in on budget. However, if the forecaster is subject to the type of controls mentioned here, then 4 'wrong' forecasts in 10 may be a few too many for the forecaster's own career progression (Figure 3.2).

Figures 3.1 and 3.2 illustrate, respectively, internal rate of return and project cost forecasts, showing in each case the areas within which **conservative** and **risk-seeking** forecasts lie. A conservative and self-preserving estimate of project cost will lie in the upper

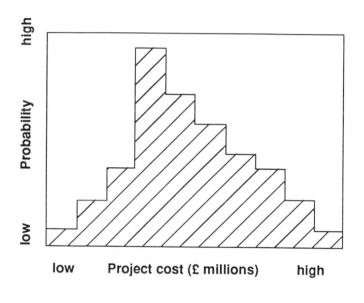

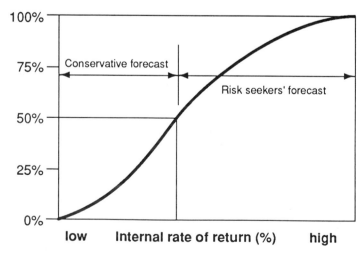

Figure 3.1 Risk attitude in forecast of return

range of possible outcomes. We may regard as risk-seeking any estimate from the lower end of the range, with a probability of being exceeded of at least 0.5. Conversely, when we consider forecasts of project return, the conservative forecaster will draw a forecast from the lower end of the range. This is a very safe forecast. It will be relatively unlikely that the project will dis-

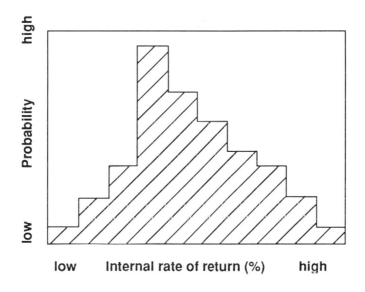

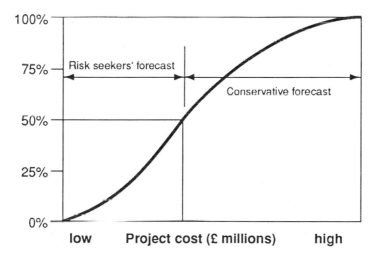

Figure 3.2 Risk attitude in forecast of costs

appoint its sponsors by producing no return or a very small return. Our choice of 0.5 as the cut-off point is purely arbitrary and for the purposes of discussion. In reality a client may choose a different cut-off, dependent on its own corporate risk attitude.

3.4.2   Differences in personal risk attitude

Biases and misinterpretation occur even in situations where the output from a cost model is reported in ways which purport to take account of risk exposure. A consultant may indicate that there is a 'good' chance that the completed project in a specific location will achieve a rent of, say, £70 per square foot. Speaking *ex ante*, probably before the site has even been purchased, the consultant knows that the project will not be complete and available for at least two years, at which time the state of the property market could be the same, better or worse than today. Similarly, an adviser may state that there is a 'reasonable' chance that a project can be completed for less than £40 million. What do these statements actually mean? The language, in itself, seems reasonably clear. However, is a 'good' chance a 9 in 10, an 8 in 10 or a 6 in 10? Is a 'reasonable' chance an 8 in 10, a 7 in 10 or a 5 in 10? These differences could be very significant to a decision maker choosing between projects or between different approaches to the same project. What is the decision maker to do? It would seem rational for the decision maker to try to deduce the influences that were acting upon the forecasters and to make adjustments for this before making decisions based on this information. Thus, 'this consultant is looking for an unblemished record leading to further work. Therefore this forecast is likely to be conservative so I shall add 10% to this estimate of project return.' This adjustment is, of course, arbitrary. The same sort of arguments could be applied to multiple single-point forecasts such as those employing the three points – most likely, optimistic and pessimistic. The precise point at which the optimistic and pessimistic values are located is a function of the risk attitude of the forecaster. As such it is unlikely to be identical to the risk attitude of the decision maker and, therefore, may lead to biased decisions. Even if the decision maker decides to adjust for the bias of the forecaster the nature of the adjustment is likely to be quite arbitrary and thus may also result in bias. Let us consider an example of what can happen in practice.

What the estimator said . . .
Assume that an estimator is just completing work on a bid for a large overseas project. The estimator has to report a **net cost estimate** to the managing director who will make the mark-up decision. The estimating team get together on the day before the bid is due to be submitted and decide that their best estimate of the net cost is $72m. This figure includes tangible and intangible costs, head office overheads and an allowance for the cost of recovering finance charges. It includes no profit, normal or otherwise. This has been arrived at by breaking the project down as indicated in Table 3.1.

Table 3.1 Deterministic estimate of net project cost

COMPONENT	COST
Materials	$25m
Labour	10m
Subcontractors	20m
Overheads and finance	12m
Supervision on site	5m
Total	$72m

What the manager thought the estimator said . . .
The manager receives this figure together with the background briefing on the project from the estimators and the planning department. The decision on mark-up is a familiar problem to the manager who is accustomed to taking calculated risks in

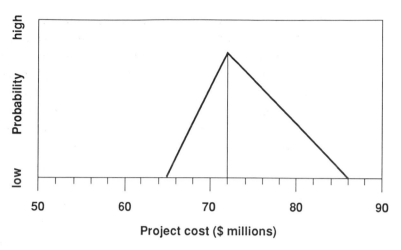

Figure 3.3 Manager's perception of the single-point estimate

order to secure work at favourable rates for the firm. The manager knows that the estimate is a **forecast** of the outturn cost should the firm win the project. Thus, for the purposes of calculation, it would be rational to assume that the estimate is the **most likely** figure drawn from a distribution which manifests some skewness at the upper end of the range. In estimates of **costs** we expect a right skew – in other words, if things go very well then the costs may be at the lower end of the range. On the other hand, if things go badly they can go very badly, so that the distribution is unlikely to be symmetrical. This is illustrated in Figure 3.3. The mental cost model of the project held in the mind of the manager is that described by the figure. The characteristics of this model are that the most likely outturn cost is $72m. The optimistic outcome is a project net cost of $65m, and the pessimistic outcome shows a cost of $86m.

What the estimator thought but did not say . . .
In a number of risk analysis workshops carried out on an earlier project it was possible to analyse, in detail, deterministic project cost estimates. This exercise involved meeting the estimating teams towards the end of the bid period when they had a quite firm deterministic idea of the net cost of the project. In a two-hour

session it was possible to carry out a detailed simulation of the project to produce a frequency histogram of possible outcomes and, from this, a cumulative probability graph. The experience of these analyses was that, when the simulation results were obtained it was usually found that the deterministic figure given earlier had been extremely conservative, with a probability of being exceeded often in the region of 0.9. This is not surprising given the long history of empirical studies demonstrating that business people have a tendency to be markedly risk-averse. Thus, for the purposes of discussion, using that datum, we may construct what our generalized estimator thought but did not say. This is illustrated in Figure 3.4 where we see that the $72m is a conservative estimate drawn from a distribution with lower and upper bounds of $59m and $79m respectively.

The amount of bias introduced is illustrated by combining Figures 3.3 and 3.4 into Figure 3.5. This is a generalized abstracted case but it illustrates well the potential for disagreement when people implicitly adopt conservative forecasting as a method of coping with certain types of managerial control of professional work. The solution to this problem is abstractly obvious although possibly difficult to implement. Forecasters should adopt methods which **explicitly** deal with both risk exposure and risk attitude.

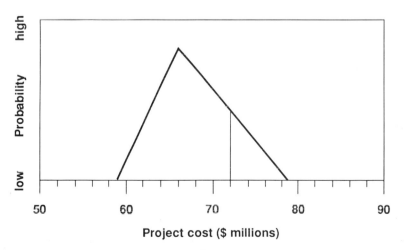

Figure 3.4 Estimator's perception of project cost

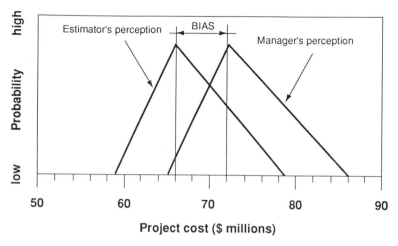

Figure 3.5 Forecasting bias

3.5 CONCLUSIONS

Unfortunately there is not a consensus in the literature on biases. The principal conclusions to be drawn from the material presented here include the following.

- There is a pattern of bias in judgements by lay people thinking intuitively about problems.
- Although there is lots of evidence of systematic error among lay people, there is much less evidence that professionals working in their own field on relatively routine tasks show biases to the same extent.
- It is suggested that if construction professionals gain an overall familiarity with the literature on biases and the details of the main findings, this should lead, in theory, to a reduction in this type of bias when they are doing their own professional work.
- The reporting of estimates and the passing of figures from one person to another leads to the introduction of biases.
- Reporting biases will never be completely eradicated until the outcome of forecasts and estimates is disconnected entirely from pay and promotional prospects. This latter may be undesirable for other reasons. The best that can be done is probably to render explicit as many assumptions as is possible, given the nature and working conditions of the organization.

- Specific steps may be taken to increase the awareness of bias and to reduce its incidence. These include:

  1. Ensure that all appropriate staff have some familiarity with the notions of personal and reporting bias.
  2. Introduce procedures to incorporate feedback loops into the filing of estimates and forecasts.
  3. Introduce procedures to ensure that as many assumptions as possible are made explicit, especially when they are assumptions about risk and uncertainty.
  4. Foster a culture of estimating and forecasting which (a) centres on explicitly dealing with risks and uncertainties across portfolios of projects and (b) accepts that some forecasts will prove to be inadequate. If forecasts are never found to be exceeded then this raises questions about the possibility of overconservative forecasting.

- Forecasts which turn out to be too high (and were thus very safe) should be treated with the same type of negative feedback as forecasts which turn out to be too low.

3.6 SUMMARY

The results of some of the most recent work on judgements and biases in estimating and forecasting are presented. This chapter sets out to help estimators to view their work more systematically and to make allowances for common human errors of judgement. Key points include a questioning of the basis of one of the more common rules of thumb. A case is presented which suggests that there is a significant chance that the figure reported in an estimate, forecast or budget for a construction project **will not even be the most likely figure** in the possible range of outcomes. It is shown that when estimators are working systematically on routine tasks they are likely to exhibit less of a tendency to bias than seems to be expected in the general public.

CHAPTER 4

RISK ATTITUDE

4.1 INTRODUCTION

In order to make a decision, we assemble information, analyse it and interpret the results. Interpretation of information or analytical results is influenced, among other things, by professional experience, the quality of our judgement, our knowledge of subjective information – which may not have been included in the analysis – and our attitude to the problem under consideration. This chapter is about personal and corporate attitudes to risk. We shall begin by returning to a theme introduced in Chapter 2 – gambler's risk aversion – and shall then present some basic ideas about the range, and apparent irrationality, of risk attitudes.

First an aside. Many readers will by now have noticed that we are almost half-way through this book and have not mentioned risk analysis techniques. This is in keeping with the objectives of the book, which include the avoidance of checklist or 'model' approaches. Our key objective is to demystify the subject and to encourage professionals to use their experience and judgement more fully. Quantitative techniques are important but it is equally important that the user of a technique be fully aware of its strengths and weaknesses, the context of the decision and the factors which influence attitude.

4.2 RISK ATTITUDE IN GAMBLING: 'CARD COUNTING'

One of the most famous contemporary professional gamblers is Dr Edward O. Thorp. Thorp is an American mathematician who – although he now specializes in playing the stock market – began his gambling career by analysing optimal strategies for beating casino 'blackjack' dealers. He was eventually banned from the premises by several casino owners. We must deduce from this that he enjoyed some success in his chosen objective. His successful approach to minimizing the risk exposure of the gambler in blackjack is worth describing.

In the game of blackjack or '21' each player (dealer included) initially receives two cards. The objective is to reach or get as near as possible to 21. Numbered cards are valued at their face value,

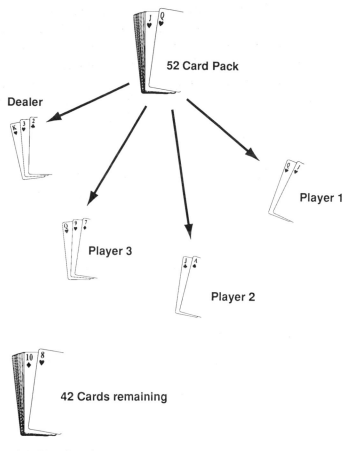

Figure 4.1 First hand

picture cards at 10 and the aces at either 1 or 11 at the player's discretion. After the initial hand of two cards each player decides to 'stick' or draw further cards. Each player may draw further cards as long as his or her total hand does not exceed 21. If the dealer or the player 'busts' (exceeds 21), the one who busts loses the bet. If neither person busts, the winner is the one closest to 21. There are some other detailed rules to the game but they are not relevant to this illustration. Thorp showed that the profit-maximizing strategy for the dealer is, in effect, a risk-minimizing strategy. The cards remaining in the pack at any given time may, on balance, be either favourable or unfavourable to the player. The pack starts off with 52 cards in a neutral position (Figure 4.1). If a relatively large number of small-value cards are drawn off in initial hands then the remaining pack will have a tendency to deal out tens and aces. This is good for the player. The opposite is also true. In other words if, after a series of hands dealt, the remaining pack has a disproportionate number of low-value cards, then this reduces the propensity of the player to win in subsequent hands (Figure 4.2). In effect, the pack is 'running against' the player at this point. Thorp's 'system' – called 'card counting' – for beating the dealer requires the player to keep a running record of the favourableness of the cards remaining in the pack.

It works as follows: Cards numbered 2 to 5 are assigned a value of +1; cards valued 6 to 9 are assigned a value of 0; tens and aces are assigned a value of −1 (Figure 4.3). As the game progresses the player observes which cards are dealt. Let us say the first hand

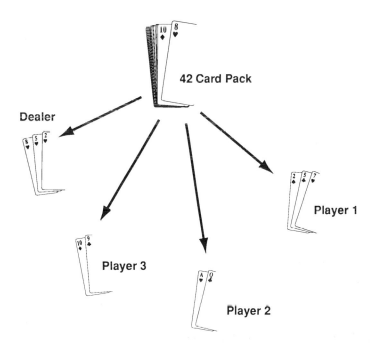

Figure 4.2 Second hand

Objective: To keep a running total of the favourableness
of the cards remaining in the pack

Card face value   Value assigned

$$
\left.\begin{array}{c}
2 \\
3 \\
4 \\
5
\end{array}\right\} \quad +1
$$

$$
\left.\begin{array}{c}
6 \\
7 \\
8 \\
9
\end{array}\right\} \quad 0
$$

$$
\left.\begin{array}{c}
10 \\
\text{Aces}
\end{array}\right\} \quad -1
$$

Figure 4.3 Card counting

2	♣	+1
10	♥	−1
Running count		0

→   *Pack remains neutral
*Small bets are appropriate

Figure 4.4 Running count 1

4	♠	+1
6	♦	0
ace	♣	−1
3	♥	+1
6	♠	0
5	♦	+1
5	♥	+1
Running count		+3

→   *Remaining cards very favourable
*pack will have propensity to deal out tens and aces
*therefore high bets are appropriate

Figure 4.5 Running count 2

consists of a two of clubs and a ten of hearts (Figure 4.4). The player counts +1, −1. The pack remains neutral. Small bets are thus still appropriate. Let us say that in subsequent hands the following cards are dealt: four of spades, six of diamonds, ace of clubs; three of hearts, six of spades, five of diamonds, five of hearts (Figure 4.5). The player counts +1, 0, −1; +1, 0, +1, +1. After this hand the running count of the pack now stands at +3. This is very favourable for the player. The pack as it now stands will have a propensity to deal out tens and aces. At this point high bets are appropriate as there is an increased likelihood of winning; or, put more accurately, the already high likelihood of losing is slightly reduced.

Card counting is a method of analysing risk and taking risks with high bets only when the odds are relatively favourable.

This system became notorious in American and European casinos. Casino owners monitored betting behaviour in a search for card counters. The system is, of course, extremely difficult to apply in practice, requiring rapid mental arithmetic during games. We mention it here merely as an illustration of the fact that apparent risk takers are often the reverse.

In the broad context of business decision making a key feature is the risk to reward ratio. Where the risks of a particular investment are high the investor will require an additional premium to make it worth while carrying such a risk. There are many examples of this principle in operation. One of the most commonly quoted is the difference between the relatively risk-free, government short-term Treasury bills issued at a fixed (low, but safe) rate of return, and the more volatile ordinary stock market shares. The stock market shows a greater rate of return over time but there are significantly higher risks, illustrated spectacularly by the world-wide market crash of October 1987. This is also the principle behind higher motor car insurance premiums for fast cars and young drivers. A similar principle applies in the financial markets for the pricing of loans for investment. If the investment project is relatively risky then the bank or finance house will add a risk premium to the interest rate. The theory of this is that, over time, the higher rate on the successful but risky loans should compensate for those few loans which become bad debts for the lender.

4.3   RISK ATTITUDE AND UTILITY THEORY

We have seen in Chapter 2 how, with a rudimentary knowledge of probability, it is possible to calculate expected monetary value (EMV) for decision outcomes. From this it is an easy step to pursue the maximization of EMV as a decision criterion when dealing with decisions under risk. However, it is frequently observed in practice that rational people will sometimes prefer an alternative to the one which offers the highest expected value. Utility theory offers a model for understanding this behaviour. Personal attitudes to risk are measured by studying individual trade-offs between gambles and certain pay-offs. Individuals are commonly assumed to fall into one of three, self-explanatory, categories: risk averse, risk seeking or risk neutral.* The comparisons are usually made by use of the so-called basic reference lottery ticket (BRLT, pronounced 'brilt'). Suppose you were lucky enough to hold in your hand a lottery ticket which gave you an even chance of winning £10 000 or nothing at all. What is the lowest price you would accept for it? The EMV of the ticket is given in the following expression:

$$EMV = (£10\,000 \times 0.5) + (£0.00 \times 0.5)$$

$$= £5000$$

Therefore a risk-neutral individual would, in theory, be willing to sell the ticket for a minimum price of £5000, which is the expected monetary value. The seller would be indifferent between the two outcomes – in other words, for this individual, the certainty equivalent of the gamble is £5000. A risk-seeking individual would want to retain the ticket for the thrill of the gamble and may not be willing to part with it until a prospective purchaser was willing to pay well over its EMV, let us say, £6500. This appears to be mathematically irrational. The risk seeker is refusing to accept, say, £6000 for a lottery ticket which has an EMV of only £5000. On

---

*It will be seen later that this is a simplification, used here only for the purpose of introducing the subject. In fact, individuals may manifest all three types of risk attitude at different points in time or, indeed, simultaneously for varying monetary and time horizons.

the other hand, a risk-averse decision maker may decide that it would be worth selling the ticket, which after all, has a 50% chance of winning nothing, for a sum less than its mathematical EMV. For example, the risk-averse individual may prefer the sure gain of £3000 to the 50% chance of either £10 000 or nothing at all. Put another way, the risk-neutral person gains equal utility from the certain payment of £5000 as from the gamble, the risk seeker gains equal utility from the certain payment of £6500 and the risk averter from £3000. The characteristics of these three types of attitude are typically plotted in Figure 4.6.

In this way utility theory explains how, but not why, rational people sometimes prefer outcomes which do not have the highest monetary value. Utility theory suggests that instead of maximizing expected monetary value, people maximize their own utility. The equation which describes the utility curve is the utility function. Utility functions vary from person to person. The utility function of an individual is unlikely to be identical to the utility function of that individual's employing organization.

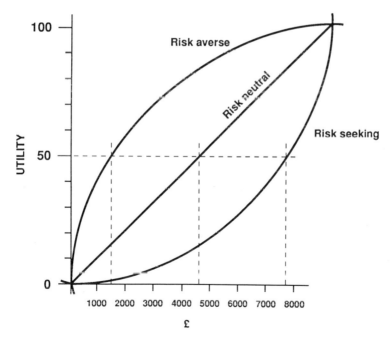

Figure 4.6 Utility curves

It has also been shown that people are not consistent and that an individual decision maker may demonstrate widely differing utility functions depending on the particular circumstances and on the size of the monetary amounts under consideration. For example, there are many people who manifest highly risk-seeking behaviour when playing poker with friends, where the maximum stake is measured in pennies, while at the same time being extremely risk averse in investing their family's savings. It would be incorrect to assume, here or elsewhere, that people are rational or consistent in their judgements about risk and uncertainty. It is for this reason that a theoretical foundation for dealing with risk which includes notions of utility theory, and rational analysis of risky real-world problems, is useful as a **prescriptive** tool which decision makers can consult or ignore as they wish.

Let us explore this theme of apparent irrationality a little further with an example from construction. Suppose we are currently negotiating two projects on behalf of a firm of contractors. The firm is currently working near capacity so we may choose only one of the two projects. The first project is a low-risk venture offering the almost certain chance of, say, £500 000 profit. The second project is rather risky, and we shall have to take design responsibility for some complex tidal protection works. Our calculations show that on the second project we face an 80% chance of generating £1 000 000 profit and a 20% chance of a £300 000 loss.

Depending on the general situation of the company a risk-averse decision would involve proceeding on project 1 while a risk-seeking decision would involve abandoning project 1 in favour of project 2 which offers the potential for greater profit. This is a rather simplistic view as the decision would depend, among other things, on the potential of a £300 000 loss sending the firm into bankruptcy. Let us assume that a loss of this size would indeed present severe problems for the firm. Then it seems prudent to proceed with the less risky project 1, which offers a fairly certain profit. It is worth noticing here that a simple mathematical analysis of the problem would point in the opposite direction. Project 1 has an EMV of £500 000. The EMV for project 2 is given by

$$\text{EMV (P2)} = (0.8 \times 1\,000\,000) + (0.2 \times -300\,000)$$

$$= £740\,000$$

Even allowing for the fact that this analysis takes no account of the seriousness of a potential £300 000 loss, we can see that a simple calculation based on risk exposure without consideration of risk attitude may point the decision maker in entirely the wrong direction.

4.4   THE ALLAIS PARADOX

This apparent paradox may be explained by a more detailed consideration of the psychology of risk. Let us consider the so-called Allais paradox (after the French economist Maurice Allais) which is credited with prompting many of the advances in the general theory of random choice and the psychology of risk. A decision maker is faced with two questions as follows:

1.   Do you prefer situation A or situation B?

  Situation A: Receive a certain £1 million
  Situation B: Receive a lottery ticket with
      (a) a 10% chance of winning £5 million
      (b) an 89% chance of winning £1 million
      (c) a 1% chance of winning nothing.

2.   Do you prefer situation C or situation D?

  Situation C: Receive a lottery ticket with
      (a) a 10% chance of winning £5 million
      (b) a 90% chance of winning nothing.
  Situation D: Receive a lottery ticket with
      (a) an 11% chance of winning £1 million
      (b) an 89% chance of winning nothing.

Alternatively, this may be presented as a decision tree (Figure 4.7).
    Over a large number of empirical studies it has been shown that very careful people, who are well aware of the probability calculus, are considered to be rational and whose personal capital is small compared to the sums involved, tend to prefer A over B **and** C over D. On the face of it, this seemed at first to be irrational. The

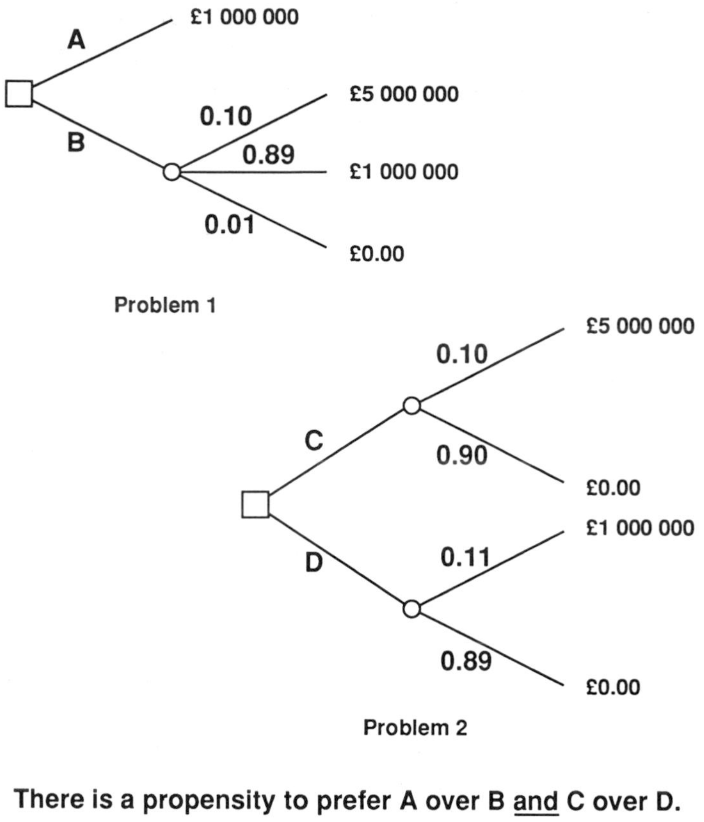

There is a propensity to prefer A over B <u>and</u> C over D.

Figure 4.7 The Allais paradox

relevant EMV values are as follows:

$$\text{EMV (A)} = \text{£1 million}$$

$$\text{EMV (B)} = \text{£1.39 million}$$

$$\text{EMV (C)} = \text{£0.5 million}$$

$$\text{EMV (D)} = \text{£0.11 million}$$

It was previously thought that a preference for A over B necessarily entailed a preference for D over C. This paradox demonstrates that people can be both risk averse **and** risk seeking, depending on the context. To be more specific, it is now known that, in general, subjects intuitively have quite a sophisticated understanding of utility which takes account of the **distribution** of utility about its mathematical expectation as well as the expected utility itself. This is the case particularly when the figures involved are large in relation to the subject's own capital.

4.5   RISK ATTITUDE: PRACTICAL IMPLICATIONS

Although it is possible to plot individual utility curves it is time consuming and difficult. Most decisions made in building economics are made by individuals or groups on behalf of private or public firms or other large institutions. Thus, to be realistic, the utility function of interest in building economics will usually be a **corporate** utility function. There is ample empirical evidence that even the simple utility curve of an individual decision maker varies quite widely over time and depends on the size of the numbers being dealt with. Owing to the cumbersome nature of the work necessary to construct these functions, the construction of corporate utility functions is not a practical possibility in most situations. Contrary to the public perception, a large proportion of business people are highly risk averse. This implies that their utility functions are concave to the origin and of the general quadratic form illustrated in Figure 4.6. Utility theory does give a well-founded starting point for a more analytical study of risk in business decisions.

4.5.1   Allowing for risk attitude

The techniques presented in Chapter 5 allow risk attitude to be considered informally. Only the risk-adjusted discount rate (RADR) contains an explicit formal adjustment for risk attitude. Risk attitude can be pursued in greater depth by plotting utility functions of decision-making individuals or by compiling 'certainty equivalent' tables. The compilation of these tables takes a lot of time and energy and their results may quickly become out of date. They are not recommended here for the practical purposes of decision making in the construction situations. Informal consideration of risk attitude should normally be sufficient as long as all assumptions are made explicit and the problems of reporting bias (see Chapter 3) are at the forefront when discussing forecasts and making decisions on the basis of reported figures.

4.6   CONCLUSIONS

The use of formal methods, based on utility theory, for dealing with risk attitude is difficult and costly. Nevertheless, utility theory has a solid theoretical foundation. A firm that can direct its staff to make decisions which are consistent with the firm's risk attitude will, over time, select better projects and make more finely tuned decisions. The research and development necessary for this is expensive and would require to be constantly reviewed. It is suggested here that much can be achieved by educating staff to increase their understanding and awareness of risk attitude and by helping them to make consistent decisions through the use of informal approaches. Thus, decisions consistent with the firm's risk attitude will be taken through **informal** analysis. In addition to being easier to undertake, informal approaches to risk attitude offer a further advantage: they respond far more rapidly to changes in the environment or in corporate attitudes to risk.

4.7   SUMMARY

This chapter is concerned with the interpretation of risk analysis and how this is influenced by personal and corporate attitudes to risk. Although no deep knowledge of mathematics is required to understand and carry out risk analysis, it is useful to be familiar with some of the basic ideas of probability, subjective probability and utility theory. This chapter introduces these ideas in a non-mathematical way and suggests some practical guidelines for taking risk attitude into account when interpreting risk analysis.

CHAPTER 5

MEASURING RISK EXPOSURE: TECHNIQUES OF RISK ANALYSIS

5.1 INTRODUCTION

5.2 TECHNIQUES
5.2.1 The risk premium
5.2.2 Sensitivity testing
5.2.3 Expected monetary value (EMV)
5.2.4 Expected net present value (ENPV)
5.2.5 EMV using a Delphi peer group
5.2.6 Risk-adjusted discount rate (RADR)
5.2.7 Detailed analysis and simulation
5.2.8 Stochastic dominance

5.3 ASSESSMENT OF THE TECHNIQUES
5.3.1 The risk premium
5.3.2 Sensitivity testing
5.3.3 EMV and ENPV methods
5.3.4 EMV using a Delphi peer group
5.3.5 Risk-adjusted discount rate (RADR)
5.3.6 Detailed analysis and simulation
5.3.7 Stochastic dominance

5.4 SUMMARY

5.1 INTRODUCTION

The choice of approach for dealing with the analysis depends on the size, type and general nature of the project or the problem being modelled, the amount and reliability of information available and the nature of the output required. The nature of the output needed will depend on the type of decisions to be made and on the particular needs of the client. Given the introductory material in the other chapters covering risk exposure, risk attitude, probability and utility, we present below examples of seven different ways of dealing with the analysis, plus a section on stochastic dominance, which is a method of assessing the results. There is some overlap among these approaches and some are unsuitable for particular situations; that is, for any given decision on a particular project at a particular point in the project schedule, there may be quite a limited choice of approach to the analysis.

- The risk premium;
- Sensitivity testing;
- Expected monetary value (EMV);
- Expected net present value (ENPV);
- EMV using a Delphi peer group;
- Risk-adjusted discount rate (RADR);
- Detailed analysis and simulation;
- Stochastic dominance.

Experienced practitioners of risk analysis and construction risk management are, rightly, quick to point out that the technique of analysis is a very small part of the overall process. Just as there is no such thing as a software-only solution to the problem of dealing rigorously with risk and uncertainty, so the **technique** used for analysis must be viewed in the context of an overall attitude of mind, which is the framework for risk management.

5.2 TECHNIQUES

5.2.1 The risk premium

Rather like Voltaire's Candide, who was excited to discover that he had been speaking **prose** all his life, the **risk premium** is commonly known in the construction industry as the **contingency fund**. There is, in this book, no intention of suggesting that risks have been ignored in construction economics and management. The opposite is the case. It would be regarded as negligent if any consultant or quantity surveyor produced an estimate or forecast for a project which did not include a contingency fund. This is testimony to the fact that risks have long been accounted for in construction as a matter of standard practice. The usual practice is to add a contingency premium to the base estimate to account for downside risks which cannot accurately be forecast at the time.

5.2.2 Sensitivity testing

Sensitivity tests measure the effect on the model output of certain specified changes in the values of input variables and parameters. It is usual to begin with a deterministic output and to iterate through the model, examining the effect of changes in the input variables and assumptions. The resultant changes in model output may be presented as tables, graphs or so-called spider diagrams. Sometimes an analyst will vary many of the input variables in sensible combinations. It would, of course, be unrealistic to decompose a model into a number of independent components and then examine what happens to the output if all the worst or best cases are added up. If the components of the model are independent, then the probability of all of the worst cases occurring simultaneously is a joint probability problem. As we saw in Chapter 2, the solution to the latter is gained by **multiplying** the individual probabilities together. Thus, if the model has three components and the probability of the worst case in each is, say, 0.1, then the probability of all three occurring simultaneously is

$$0.1 \times 0.1 \times 0.1 = 0.001$$

This implies that where the probability of each of the worst cases individually is 1 in 10, the joint probability of all three occurring simultaneously is 1 in 1000. Therefore, caution needs to be exercised in sensitivity testing if variables are to be tested in combination.

Described in this way, sensitivity testing can appear to be a crude tool. In fact, sensitivity testing, used in a sophisticated manner, can convey an extremely useful picture of a project/investment decision under dynamic real-world conditions. Consider the following example, which is an appraisal of a proposed rehabilitation and redevelopment scheme in London. The project involves the rehabilitation of an eighteenth-century church crypt to provide a museum and restaurant, and the redevelopment of the surrounding church yard to include speculative office space and a small (fee-paying) nursery school. The details of the original investment appraisal were based on four phases of construction, occupied twice that number of pages of calculations, and are not germane to the present discussion. The sensitivity analysis consisted of only three tables, as shown.

From Table 5.1 it can be seen that no profit would be made at all if, other things being equal, the capital value of the offices were to fall by 25% on the original assumption. Similarly, the building period would have to increase from one to two-and-a-half years, or the building costs would have to increase by 37% from £89 to £122, for the profit to be entirely eroded. The table considers one variable at a time. Tables 5.2 and 5.3 consider three scenarios with changes in sensible combinations of the input variables.

Table 5.3 shows the *ex ante* assumptions about a range of scenarios by taking, in each case, a set of sensible assumed values for each of the important variables. The table indicates that the original scenario for this project appraisal was risk averse in its assumptions about capital growth on the completed project. On building costs it was slightly risk seeking as it had made no allowance for building cost escalation during the development period. The realistic scenario allows for both a 5% capital growth in the value of the completed project and for a building cost escalation of 7.5% per annum. This has been combined with a three-month void period before the offices part of the project is

Table 5.1   Sensitivity test: St Alfege's redevelopment

VARIABLE	CHANGE IN VARIABLE TO ELIMINATE PROFIT	NEW VALUE OF VARIABLE (APPROX.)	ORIGINAL VALUE OF VARIABLE
Capital value of offices per square foot	25%	£169	£255
Building costs (including ancillary costs p.s.f.)	37%	£122 (office cost)	£89 (office cost)
Finance rate p.a.	302%	74.4% p.a.	18.5% p.a.
Building period	350%	4.5 years	1 year
Period before offices sold	700%	2 years	0.25 year

sold. The pessimistic scenario looks at a period of high inflation and high interest rates with a void period of nine months before sale. This is clearly a recessionary view of the market. It is a description of a market which has overheated, run into high inflation and interest rates, oversupply of space and a decline in confidence. This is a quite realistic view of the beginning of a significant downturn in the property market. The optimistic view taken in this appraisal does seem, with hindsight, to be quite optimistic. It combined assumptions of continued strong growth in the capital value of the finished project with low inflation and interest rates. These are by no means the best or worst cases; they were, on the whole, quite realistic combinations of variables in the market conditions prevailing at the time.

Table 5.2   Sensitivity test: scenarios

VARIABLE	ORIGINAL SCENARIO	OPTIMISTIC	REALISTIC	PESSIMISTIC
Growth in capital value	0	7%	5%	1%
Building cost increase	0	6% p.a.	7.5% p.a.	10% p.a.
Finance rate	18.5%	16.5%	18.5%	20%
Building period	12 months	9 months	12 months	15 months
Period before sale of offices	3 months	No delay	3 months	9 months
Contingencies	5%	5%	5%	5%

Table 5.3   Sensitivity test: changes in model output

OUTCOME	ORIGINAL SCENARIO	OPTIMISTIC	REALISTIC	PESSIMISTIC
Residual profit	£749 540	£879 460	£779 650	£222 600
% of capital value	24.73%	27.12%	24.5%	7.2%
% of total costs	32.86%	37.21%	32.45%	7.8%
Increase over original estimate	0	17.33%	4.02%	−70.3%

5.2.3   Expected monetary value (EMV)

The expected monetary value (EMV) approach takes the testing of scenarios one stage further by considering also the subjective probability of occurrence of each scenario. In this approach, the model is broken down into a number of components and each one is examined separately in terms of a range of scenarios with their associated probabilities. These may be as simple as best case/worst case or as complex as a large number of scenarios ranging from optimistic to pessimistic. For example, consider the case of forward planning for a district health authority. In order for the health authority to make a bid for central funds, a budget estimate is required for a clinic. Thus, the neighbourhood is known but not the actual site. The budget for bidding purposes might be broken down into only three components: substructure (affected by the eventual ground conditions), superstructure (affected by the detailed design decisions) and inflation (affected by prevailing economic/market conditions). Combinations of best and worst cases may be considered. It is important, though, to avoid simply combining all the best and worst cases in order to produce the extremes of possible outcome. The latter error produces answers – as we have seen – that are too pessimistic on the upper bound, and too optimistic on the lower. The expected outcomes approach is a more powerful and robust way of examining separate sources of risk. This involves assigning probabilities to discrete outcome states and combining the results to give an EMV (Figure 5.1). This gives a 'risk-adjusted' outcome. In the case of this example, the authority may choose to examine three scenarios for each of the

$$\text{EMV (sub)} = (0.2\times720k) + (0.5\times800k) + (0.3\times1000k) = £856\,070$$
$$\text{EMV (sub)} = (0.2\times1800k) + (0.6\times2000k) + (0.2\times2500k) = £2\,060\,000$$
$$\text{EMV (inf)} = (0.2\times9\%) + (0.5\times12\%) + (0.3\times16\%) = 12.6\%$$

$$\text{EMV (project)} = [\text{EMV(sub)} + \text{EMV(sup)}] \times \text{EMV (inf)}$$
$$\Rightarrow \text{EMV (project)} = [856\,070 + 2\,060\,000] \times 1.126$$
$$\Rightarrow \text{EMV (project)} \ £3\,282\,500$$

Figure 5.1   The EMV for the project

Table 5.4 Probabilistic scenario analysis

		OPTIMISTIC	MOST LIKELY	PESSIMISTIC
Substructure	Outcome	£720 000	£800 000	£1 000 000
	Probability	0.2	0.5	0.3
Superstructure	Outcome	£1 800 000	£2 000 000	£2 500 000
	Probability	0.2	0.6	0.2
Inflation	Outcome	9%	12%	16%
	Probability	0.2	0.5	0.3

components of the cost model. These could be as simple as optimistic, most likely and pessimistic. A probability is attached to each scenario for each component of the model. Table 5.4 shows typical values for a problem of this type.

5.2.4 Expected net present value (ENPV)

Expected monetary values can be applied in a wide variety of situations. Consider the following example of a simple model for investment appraisal. Geoff's Joinery Ltd are considering the purchase of new machinery for the production of prefabricated roof trusses for low-rise housing. The capital cost of the equipment and installation is £0.5 million. The annual income from the venture depends on the utilization of the machinery which is, in turn, dependent on the state of the house-building industry. The industry is currently on a minor upturn. Confidence is returning after a period of recession but there are political and economic uncertainties and there is, as yet, no clear evidence that the upturn will be sustained. On this basis the managing director has calculated three scenarios, as indicated in Table 5.5. The annual incomes are net of all costs of production.

Geoff's Joinery Ltd normally use an 8% discount rate in investment appraisal. This represents the firm's view of its long-term real (inflation-adjusted) cost of capital. The project NPVs were then calculated on this basis for the three states. Finally, an assessment

Table 5.5   Net income projections

	STATE OF THE INDUSTRY		
Year	Declines (£)	Remains steady (£)	Growth accelerates (£)
Net income: Year 1	170 000	180 000	200 000
Year 2	150 000	200 000	250 000
Year 3	150 000	200 000	250 000
Year 4	150 000	200 000	250 000

Table 5.6   States, probabilities and NPVs

STATE	PROBABILITY	NPV (£)
Steady state	0.6	142 680
Growth	0.2	280 200
Decline	0.2	14 420

of the probability of each of the three outcomes was made. This information is displayed in Table 5.6.

On the basis of this information the firm calculates its **expected NPV (ENPV)** as follows:

			£
Steady	£142 680 × 0.6	=	85 608
Growth	£280 200 × 0.2	=	56 040
Decline	£14 420 × 0.2	=	2 884
ENPV		=	144 532

The EMV approach may be used in a variety of settings. ENPV is useful in investment and development appraisal. The example given here is for investment appraisal, the same approach could be used for development appraisal of new building or infrastructure projects.

5.2.5 EMV using a Delphi peer group

This method utilizes a formal Delphi group and is designed to pool the expertise of many professionals in such a way as to gain access to their knowledge and to their technical skills while removing the influences of seniority, hierarchies and personalities on the derived forecast. The method is named after the oracle at Delphi in ancient Greece. In this method a group of experts is identified. The members of the group are kept physically separate, so there is no personal interaction among them. The coordinator asks each member of the group to make a forecast and a subjective probability estimate for the relevant components of the project under consideration. The coordinator receives and summarizes these estimates, and the summary is given as feedback to all members of the group. The names of members are not attached to any individual forecasts. The group members are then asked to amend their forecasts in the light of the information in the summary. The new forecasts are summarized and this is communicated to all members. This process of forecast, amendment and feedback continues until either there is a consensus or the members of the group no longer wish to amend their forecasts. In either case, the final result is the Delphi forecast. The physical separation is designed to nullify the effects of strong personalities and other undesirable consequences of personal interaction. Of course, this is not to say that personal interaction produces only negative results. The Delphi method is merely a way of focusing on the task and ironing out the biases of poor metacognition and overconfidence which may encroach on forecasts. There is no doubt that this is a powerful method of assessing important projects at the budget and feasibility stage. For many projects it could easily be conducted, using electronic mail, over the course of an afternoon. The group members would have no need to be in the same building or even in the same country.

In the case of our examples of the library (in Chapter 2) and the new equipment decisions above, the results of the Delphi forecast would be a table of outcomes and probabilities in the form presented, for example, in Tables 5.5 and 5.6.

5.2.6 Risk-adjusted discount rate RADR

RADR is an intuitive method of dealing with risk and is commonly used in banking and business. The method is, unfortunately, not well understood in construction and property circles. RADR is very simple to use and offers a method of dealing with both risk exposure **and** risk attitude. The method works by decomposing the discount rate used in the cost model into component parts. Begin with a risk-free rate of interest. Many decision makers regard the long-term return on government bonds as a good proxy for a 'risk-free' rate of return. For estimated **benefit** streams in the life of a project the rate is adjusted upwards to take account of the normal risk encountered in this type of investment. A second adjustment is made to reflect the particular perceived risk of a specific project or investment. The effect of these upward adjustments to the discount rate is to **reduce the calculated present value of future income**. Hence, they render the project/investment less desirable. The project now has a higher hurdle to surmount in order to avoid being rejected. For example, a decision maker may typically add 3% to reflect the risk of his or her business and then class projects into risk categories. These categories could be as simple as low risk, medium risk and high risk with, respectively, adjustments of 1%, 3% and 5%. The size of the adjustment reflects the degree of risk exposure for the type of project and the risk attitude of the decision maker. A risk-seeking decision maker may decide that high-risk projects should receive an adjustment of only 3.5%. This lower adjustment for the same degree of risk exposure reflects a different risk attitude on the part of that particular decision maker.

A further complication arises when attempting to use RADR in life-cycle costing or any other model where there are subsequent **cost** as well as benefit streams in the life of the project. These subsequent cost streams would typically represent maintenance, renewal, replacement, repair or cleaning and operating costs. The objective of the adjustment for risk is to render the project less desirable. However, slavish application to the project costs of the risk-adjusted rate for benefit streams would completely distort the analysis by rendering the project **more** attractive. Under a higher discount rate the present value of future outgoings would be understated. This feature of RADR is rarely stated in the construction literature.

In summary, for **benefit** streams the risk adjustments are an **increasing** function of risk. For **cost** streams the risk adjustments are a **decreasing** function of risk. In other words, the discount rate on cost streams should be reduced to take account of increasing risk and uncertainty.

This has the further implication that in order to use RADR effectively in many building-cost models it will be necessary to have a range of discount rates for one project or one investment decision. At the very least it will be necessary to have two rates, one for benefits and one for costs. It may further be thought useful to use different risk-adjusted rates for different components of the problem. It may, for example, be thought that in the life of a particular project there will be considerably more uncertainty about future energy costs of services operation than labour costs of cleaning and maintenance. In this case it may be appropriate to use two cost-stream discount rates. This may be summarized as follows:

$$RADR_iP = RFR + RA_1 + RA_2$$

where $RADR_iP$ is the ith RADR for that particular project or cost model; RFR is the risk-free discount rate; RA_1 is the risk adjustment to reflect the normal risk of the business carried on by the decision maker; and RA_2 is the risk adjustment to reflect special risk exposure for this project/component of a project and the attitude taken to it by the decision maker.

We have introduced the subscript 'i' to the RADR to recognize that for any given model, project or investment decision there may be a number of RADRs, with, at the very least, one each for the cost and the benefit streams. Typically, the adjustments RA_1 and RA_2 would be positive figures for benefit streams and negative for cost streams. This treatment is slightly simplified by using the addition approach for adjusting the base risk-free rate.

Table 5.7   RADR appraisal for Geoff's Joinery Ltd

$$\text{RADR}_1 \text{ (benefits)} = 7+2+1 = 10\%$$
$$\text{RADR}_2 \text{ (costs)} = 7-2-1 = 4\%$$

				RADR=4%	
	GROSS	RADR=10%			
	INCOME	DCF	COSTS	DCF	NCF
YEAR	(£)	(£)	(£)	(£)	(£)
0			(500 000)	(500 000)	(500 000)
1	580 000	527 220	(400 000)	(384 800)	142 420
2	600 000	495 600	(400 000)	(370 000)	125 600
3	600 000	450 600	(400 000)	(355 600)	95 000
4	600 000	409 800	(400 000)	(342 000)	67 800
	NPV (risk adjusted)				(69 180)

Consider, as an example, the decision to invest in new machinery by Geoff's Joinery Ltd. Let us consider, in this case, the steady-state scenario. Assume a risk-free rate of, say, 7%. The normal bank premium for lending to this firm is, say, 2%. Assume that the current proposal to extend the area of production into prefabricated roof trusses is seen as a natural extension of the firm's other work, and thus attracts a low-risk premium of a further 1%. The RADRs are given in Table 5.7.

Table 5.7 displays the results of the RADR appraisal. This appraisal indicates that given the risk loading of the firm and the project, and the attitude to risk taken by the bank and the firm, the project does not produce a positive NPV. In this form the project would not be accepted as an investment.

5.2.7   Detailed analysis and simulation

Using this method the estimator need no longer be restricted to conventional estimates. If the estimator tends to opt for 'safe' figures (i.e. with room to manoeuvre if something goes wrong) then the result will be an overconservative estimate. On the other hand, if the 'most likely' figure is adopted then all the estimator's accumulated experience and judgement about other possibilities is lost when the results are added up to one single figure. By using computer simulation it is possible to carry through the estimate a complete judgement about the range of each variable and the relative likelihood of each value in that range (Figure 5.2). This judgement is made in the form of a probability distribution defined by the estimator, which reflects the sum of his or her knowledge about that variable. Using a simulation program (probably built on the back of a spreadsheet such as Lotus) the project is 'built' many times. Thus, we are able to observe the effect of the combined probabilities. On each 'pass' through the project, the program selects for each item a cost which is chosen from the input

Figure 5.2 Probabilistic forecast

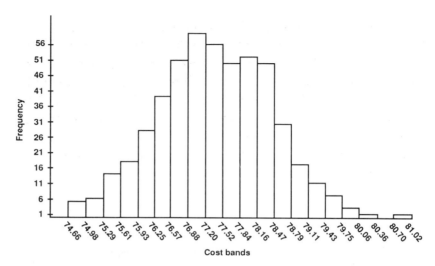

Figure 5.3 Probability distribution

distribution for that item. The simulation results in a statistical sample of projects with identical probabilistic characteristics, each of which has had a different outcome. Analysis of this sample enables us to attach some numeric evaluation to the degree of risk in the estimate.

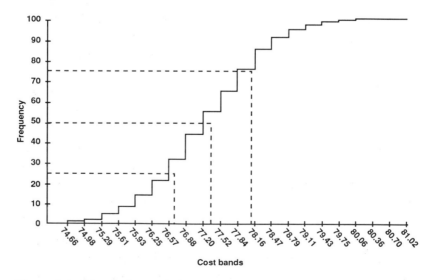

Figure 5.4 Cumulative probability distribution

In the example shown here, the estimate was simulated 500 times and the results are displayed in Figures 5.3 and 5.4. In this case we can see that it is very probable that the original estimate of $76.505m will be exceeded. This approach enables a numeric evaluation of the degree of risk contained in the estimate. The problem has been constructed in a way that makes use of the full range of knowledge of the estimators concerning the most likely, best and worst cases for each of the components of the project. The simulation approach ensures that each variable receives its proper weighting in the final analysis.

When an estimate or forecast is prepared deterministically in practice, and is then subjected to a risk analysis and simulation, the outcome is frequently the opposite of the example shown here. When construction project forecasts are analysed in this way, the original deterministic forecast is often found to have been highly risk averse, with perhaps only a 1 in 10 chance of being exceeded. The reasons for this are examined in detail in Chapters 3 and 4.

Choice of distribution

The choice of input distribution is not based upon a search for the 'true' distribution for the variable in question but on the objective of modelling the estimator's perception of the range and probability of the likely outcomes for it. We are in the realm, not of repeatable statistical assessment, but of subjective definitions of probability. Therefore, the distributions we choose to work with in practical situations need to have certain desired characteristics. They should be relatively easy to understand and should have clear cut-off points. Most estimators will be able to state reasonably clearly that the cost or time for a particular variable will never exceed X or be less than Y. Therefore, it is useful if the distribution actually cuts the X-axis at those points. It is also useful if the people doing the risk analysis do not need a refresher course in statistics. For these reasons the very simple distributions illustrated in Figures 5.5 to 5.10 are recommended for practical use in risk analysis on most construction projects. The distributions are quite powerful. They have been shown through experience of many projects – including undersea oil and gas and large defence projects – to produce robust models of risk.

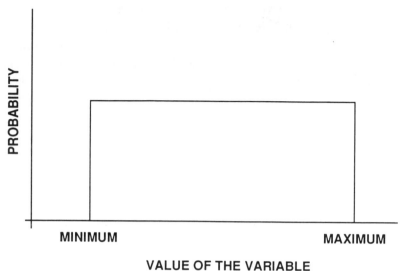

Figure 5.5 Uniform distribution

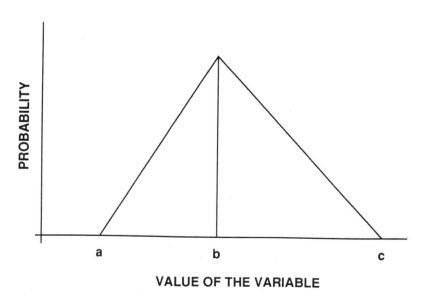

Figure 5.6 Triangular distribution

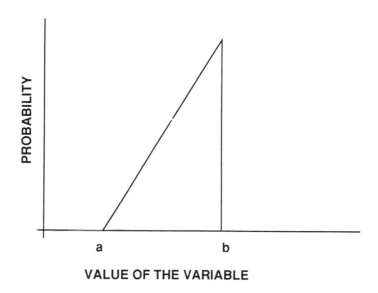

Figure 5.7 Triangular distribution

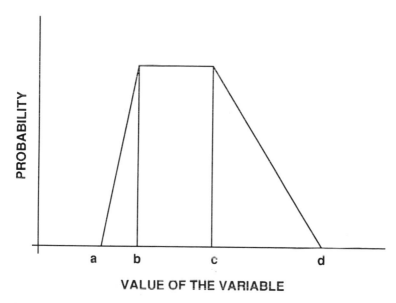

Figure 5.8 Trapezoidal distribution

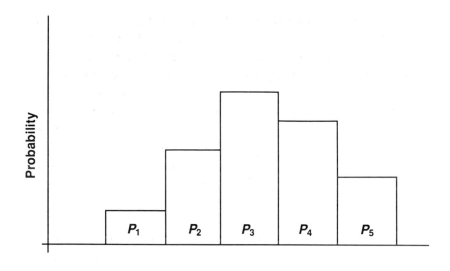

Figure 5.9 Step-rectangular distribution

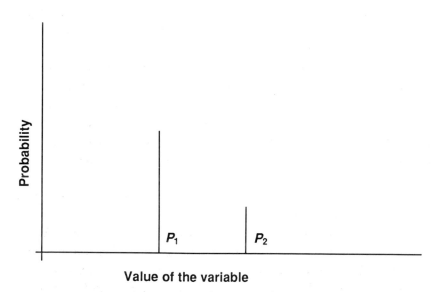

Figure 5.10 Discrete distribution

There is leeway to be somewhat flexible in the choice of input distribution as it has been shown that errors in these distributions are ameliorated by the effect of the Central Limit Theorem. The Central Limit Theorem implies that when a range of distribution shapes is entered and simulated many times, there will, as the number of simulations increases, be a tendency for the output distribution to tend to the normal shape. The precise choice of input distribution is not as important as the problem of correlation among the subsystems of the project model. It is important either to choose to analyse sources of risk which are reasonably independent or to expend a lot of time dealing with the connections between subsystems.

The distributions themselves are self-explanatory. In eliciting subjective probabilities and the parameters of the illustrated distributions, care should be taken to ensure that there are consistent rules for defining most likely, maxima and minima figures.

Correlations and independence

Experimental work by the World Bank in the early 1970s showed clearly that greater distortion of the results was produced by inadequacies in dealing with correlation than by errors in defining input distributions. For this reason it is important to be aware of the minutiae of the software being used to do the simulation. Most of the smaller programs and many of the more expensive ones do not deal with correlation. Some of the larger project management programs, which tend to simulate networks, claim to be able to deal with correlation but the detail of how strongly the links are defined is left to the user. Therefore, users need to be quite sophisticated in their understanding of probabilistic project models.

Correlation may be dealt with in this manner. Assume that activity P is dependent on the outcome of an earlier activity, say, activity K. The program should allow for this to be flagged when entering the basic simulation model. For activity P a number of different distributions are entered, each one contingent upon a specific type of result from activity K. Now, in the simulation when it is time to draw a number for activity P, the program checks back to read the result drawn for activity K during the same pass.

Reading this result the program then decides which of the range of distributions for P is now appropriate, given the outcome of activity K. For example, the results of K could be banded into three different sections. A lower band producing a very optimistic result, a middle band and a higher band producing a pessimistic result. In this case we could enter three distributions to activity P, one for each of the three cases. The correlation may be positive, where a good result in K implies a good result in P, or negative, where a good result in K implies a bad result in P.

However, it is also the case that the majority of all construction projects can be adequately simulated using very simple and inexpensive software. Detailed simulation of project activity networks is sometimes carried out for aerospace, defence and large undersea oil and gas exploration projects, but these are all much bigger, more heterogeneous and more risky than most construction projects.

5.2.8   Stochastic dominance

Comparing projects on the basis of a single-point single criterion, such as project cost, benefit to cost ratio, or internal rate of return, is a straightforward task. If, however, the project has been estimated using a simulation approach to produce a probabilistic result, then the task of comparing one project with another becomes more complex. Sometimes, by superimposing the probability density functions (PDFs) and the cumulative distribution function, it will be clear which project has stochastic dominance. In the example illustrated here we are considering the life-cycle cost of two projects. Visual examination of the PDF graph (Figure 5.11) will indicate that project 1 has a lower mean cost than project 2.

The variances seem similar on both projects. The cumulative distribution function (CDF) graph shows that for any chosen level of life cycle there is a higher likelihood that it will be achieved on project 1 than on project 2 (Figure 5.12).

Project 1 enjoys a clear stochastic dominance over project 2. In the case of projects 3 and 4 the outcome is much more ambiguous. However, it is clear that project 3, as well as having the lower cost, also has a smaller variance. Project 3 has stochastic dominance

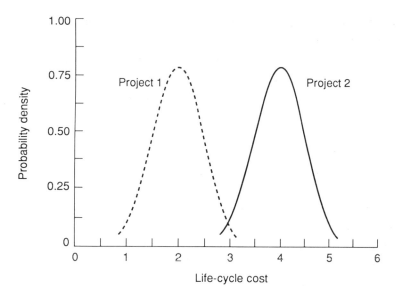

Figure 5.11 Probability density functions of the life-cycle cost for projects 1 and 2

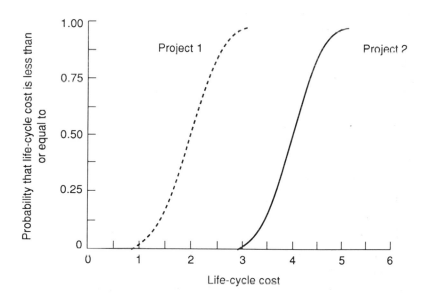

Figure 5.12 Cumulative distribution functions of the life-cycle costs for projects 1 and 2

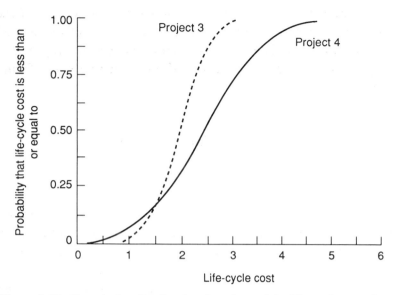

Figure 5.13 Cumulative distribution functions of the life-cycle costs for projects 3 and 4

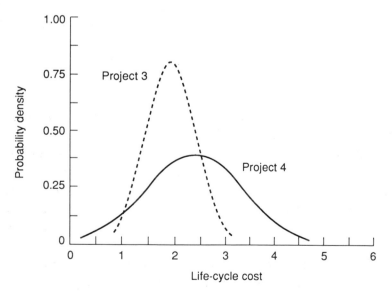

Figure 5.14 Superimposed probability density functions of the life-cycle costs for projects 3 and 4

over project 4 (Figure 5.13). What would be the outcome if the graphs were illustrating expected return rather than life-cycle cost? Then we would be faced with a situation where the project with the greater return, project 4, also had the greater variance (Figure 5.14).

5.3   ASSESSMENT OF THE TECHNIQUES

5.3.1   The risk premium

The risk premium is more commonly known as the **contingency fund** among UK professionals and as a **conservative estimate** in North America. The bigger the premium, the more certain we are that a project which is estimated to be worth while will in fact be so. The risk premium is a rather coarse instrument which combines all the independent sources of risk. It does not explicitly take account of risk attitude. It is really only suitable when the decision maker will suffer a penalty for a price forecast which turns out to be too low, but no negative sanction at all for a forecast which turns out to be too high. This has the implication that the use of the risk premium could lead to the rejection of projects which are economic.

5.3.2   Sensitivity testing

Sensitivity tests measure the impact on the project outcome of changes in the values of input variables about which there is some uncertainty. There are several advantages to the use of sensitivity tests. They are quick and easy to use. They require little information and can usually be carried out by hand. They fully recognize uncertainty in the input variables. They show how the output will be influenced by changes in the input variables either singly or in combination.

There are also several limitations with the use of sensitivity tests. They take no account of the **likelihood** of the range of input or output. Therefore they do not give a **probabilistic** picture of risk exposure. There is no explicit method of allowing for risk attitude.

Some people say that the results of sensitivity tests are at best ambiguous and at worst misleading. They are ambiguous because they do not suggest how likely it is that their pessimistic or optimistic results will occur, for example. They are misleading when some analysts take a number of worst or best case values of input variables and calculate the effect on the output. Such combinations are extremely unlikely in the real world and this type of test would produce exaggerated results both on the optimistic and on the pessimistic bounds.

5.3.3   EMV and ENPV methods

EMV methods are suitable for a range of applications. EMVs may be calculated, for example, for budget figures, for tender price forecasts, for rates of project return, or for project completion dates. The advantages of EMV methods are that they solve some of the limitations of sensitivity tests. They explicitly allow for the probability of change in input values. They produce a risk-adjusted outcome.

The limitations of EMV methods revolve around the nature of probability itself. It is possible that EMVs may not give the best practical advice for a specific project decision. EMVs suggest that over the long run on many projects of similar size and characteristics the result will have a propensity to be $X. This in no way gives specific advice about the actual project in hand. EMV should only be used as a decision criterion if it is used consistently over many similar sized projects.

5.3.4   EMV using a Delphi peer group

The addition of the Delphi group to the EMV method adds a further advantage and also a limitation. The advantage is that the Delphi group is a well-recognized method of getting the most out of a group of experts in a forecasting situation. With tolerable success it removes the unhelpful aspects of working with a group and takes advantage of the positive features of having access to more than one set of judgements. The limitation which it introduces is that it requires additional resources and time to operate.

A group of experts needs to be briefed on the project and then assembled to carry out the exercise, but they do not have to be assembled in one place. It is possible for a Delphi group to be run on an electronic conference basis. The only disadvantage is that the people involved need to clear a window of time more or less simultaneously in order to take part. The use of a Delphi approach should be considered where it is important to consult more than one expert and where the project or project risks are identified to be of sufficient size to warrant the additional effort.

5.3.5 Risk-adjusted discount rate (RADR)

The central advantage of RADR is that it offers a way of simultaneously taking account of both risk attitude and risk exposure. The technique is easy to understand and easy to calculate. Among its limitations are: (1) it is not suitable specifically for construction budgeting; (2) there is no explicit method for calculating the risk adjustments which seem rather informal and difficult to justify on any logical basis; and (3) although the risk adjustments take account of both risk exposure and risk attitude, it is not feasible to disentangle one from the other.

5.3.6 Detailed analysis and simulation

Detailed analysis and simulation offer a number of advantages. The resultant probability density and cumulative distribution functions are a powerful measure of project risk exposure. The results also allow for the informal incorporation of risk attitude by the decision maker who has to decide the level of uncertainty to accept as part of a valid forecast. The method requires very little knowledge of mathematics and can cope with a large number of types of input distribution, thus giving the flexibility to model precisely the perceptions of uncertainty surrounding all of the input variables. It is possible to deal with correlation between components of the analysis, although this requires a more sophisticated piece of software.

The disadvantages of the technique are: (1) it relies on the use of a computer and, therefore, software has to be purchased or written; and (2) each analysis needs to be structured carefully either to decompose into relatively independent subsystems or to take into account the correlation between them.

5.3.7   Stochastic dominance

Stochastic dominance is not a technique of analysis, it is really a method of assessing the results. Its principal advantage is that it offers a way of comparing probabilistic results. The method is largely informal and the result chosen may depend on personal risk attitude which is again exercised informally by viewing the graphs.

5.4   SUMMARY

This chapter presents seven methods of treating the analysis of risk. These approaches are appropriate in a variety of different situations in the context of construction projects. They cover the following types of decision: feasibility, budgeting, forecasting and project management. The methods presented are: the risk premium, sensitivity testing, expected monetary value (EMV), expected net present value (ENPV), EMV using Delphi peer groups, risk-adjusted discount rate (RADR) and detailed analysis and simulation. The chapter concludes with an assessment of the usefulness of each approach.

CHAPTER 6

CASE HISTORIES AND WORKED EXAMPLES

LIVERPOOL JOHN MOORES UNIVERSITY
Aldham Roberts L.R.C.
TEL. 051 231 3701/3684

6.1 INTRODUCTION

If you have started to work through this book by beginning with this chapter on worked examples, please think again. If you have skipped Chapter 1 you will not know that one of this book's objectives is to help the reader to develop good judgement for approaching risk analysis of projects in a variety of settings and for a wide range of project types. An important aspect of this objective is to avoid getting locked into a mechanistic or 'checklist' approach to quantitative analysis. If you already have a good knowledge of probability calculations then you may not have missed anything too important by skipping Chapter 2. Chapters 3 and 4 presented important psychological factors which influence professional judgements on projects, data and attitudes to risk. Chapter 5 gave an introduction to each technique, accompanied by an assessment of its strengths and weaknesses. No construction professional bound by the normal duty of care should use any quantitative technique without complete knowledge of its limitations. If you are comfortable about all of the above and still wish to commence here, then go ahead.

6.2   THE GOH KEE CONSTRUCTION CO.

A specialist contractor in Hong Kong is trying to evaluate the risks associated with different strategies that could be adopted in a volatile market. Goh Kee Construction Co. specializes in concrete works and is, at the time of the analysis, operating at near capacity. The marketing director of the company anticipates that the market for concrete works will increase by 15% during the next 12 months. The board must decide how to react to this change in demand. Three strategies are being considered by the board:

S1   Purchase new plant
S2   Institute overtime working
S3   Continue to work at capacity and let rivals or new firms satisfy the increased demand

The contribution that each strategy will make to profits over the next 12 months is estimated to be as follows:

- Purchasing new plant will lead to an increase in profits of HK$2m
- Overtime working will lead to a profit increase of HK$1.2m
- Continuing to work at capacity will yield HK$0.8m over the period

These values are estimated under the assumption that the market grows by 15%. However, the marketing director admits that two other outcomes are also possible: (1) demand may fall if there is an increase in the use of steel frame construction; (2) demand will remain unchanged. A decision matrix can be constructed to show this information (Figure 6.1). The options are shown in rows and the factors or states of the market are shown in columns.

What decision should the board take? If we can assign probabilities to the various outcomes then we can work out the EMVs. For the Goh Kee Construction Co. we need the probabilities associated with changes in market demand (Table 6.1). This gives us the information needed to calculate the expected values. The EMV is given by multiplying the probability by the pay-off. Thus, for

Options		Factors		
		15% rise	Stable	10% fall
	S1	HK$2.0m	HK$0.4m	0
	S2	HK$1.2m	HK$0.6m	HK$0.2m
	S3	HK$0.8m	HK$0.6m	HK$0.2m
				Outcomes

Figure 6.1 Goh Kee Construction Co.: decision matrix

Table 6.1   Goh Kee: outcomes and probabilities

MARKET OUTCOME	PROBABILITY
15% rise	0.6
Stable	0.3
10% fall	0.1

Table 6.2   Goh Kee: pay-offs for strategy S1

FACTOR	PAY-OFF	×	PROBABILITY	=	FMV
15% rise	2.0	×	0.6	=	1.20
Stable	0.4	×	0.3	=	0.12
10% fall	0	×	0.1	=	0
Total				=	1.32

Table 6.3	Goh Kee: strategies	
STRATEGY		EMV
S1	New plant	HK$1.32m
S2	Overtime	HK$0.92m
S3	Existing level	HK$0.68m

strategy S1, purchasing new plant, the calculation of EMV is shown in Table 6.2. The same process can be repeated for strategies S2 and S3. This yields the respective expected values for all three strategies. This leads us to favour approach S1 because it has the highest expected value. There is, however, more information that we could use to analyse these strategies further.

The variability of returns is also important, and can be used as a measure of the degree of risk. This measure of risk can be found by using the standard deviation. The standard deviation is given

Table 6.4   Goh Kee: variance and standard deviation for strategy S1

OUTCOME	EMV	DEVIATION	$D^2 \times$ PROBABILITY	TOTAL
2.0	1.32	+0.68	0.4642×0.6	= 0.27744
0.4	1.32	−0.92	0.8464×0.3	= 0.25392
0	1.32	−1.32	1.7424×0.1	= 0.17424
Variance				= 0.7056
Standard deviation				= 0.84

Table 6.5   Goh Kee: coefficients of variation

STRATEGY	EMV	COEFFICIENT OF VARIATION*
S1	HK$1.32m	0.64
S2	HK$0.92m	0.39
S3	HK$0.68m	0.27

*Coefficient of variation=Standard deviation/EMV

by the square root of the variance. The variance in statistics is given by the squared deviation of each pay-off from its EMV multiplied by the probability of that outcome. The standard deviation for strategy S1 is given in Table 6.4.

We now have two pieces of information. Since higher EMVs will tend to be associated with higher values for standard deviation we can use the coefficient of variation, which shows the proportionate deviation, i.e. the degree of risk (Table 6.5).

Table 6.5 shows that S1 is the most risky strategy but has the highest EMV. Any decision made now will depend upon the decision maker's attitude to risk.

6.3 A TRANSPORT INFRASTRUCTURE INVESTMENT APPRAISAL

Rathmines PLC, is a large multidivisional firm with interests in mining, property and civil engineering construction in the transport and energy sectors. The firm's board is currently considering two alternative transport investments in western Europe. Both projects are based on Build Operate Transfer (BOT) arrangements. The projects are being considered over a six-year time horizon. The first alternative is a toll bridge segment for a major orbital motorway. The second is a 25% share in a new section being added to a mass transit railway system, 70% of which is underground. In projects of this size, a major risk analysis would be carried out. The example below is highly simplified and merely demonstrates the mechanics of how the project ENPVs could be calculated.

Although this example is greatly oversimplified, it is at least one increment more realistic than the Geoff's Joinery Ltd example which was used to illustrate ENPV in Chapter 5. That example only considered one alternative (if there is such a thing). Discounted net present value calculations are only meaningful in the context of a set of mutually exclusive alternatives – which we have in the following example.

Project: Orbital Toll Bridge vs RTS Rapid Transit System – investment appraisal

---

1. Incoming cash flows are shown net of maintenance and general operating costs including intangibles.
2. Outgoing cash flows are shown gross, including all legal and financial fees.
3. Discount rate = 6%

Details of the orbital toll bridge are given in Table 6.6; the rapid transit system is detailed in Table 6.7.

Table 6.6 Orbital toll bridge

	Most likely scenario (operating at near capacity) Probability=0.8		Pessimistic scenario (Based on Delphi estimate) Probability=0.2	
YEAR	CASH FLOW	DISCOUNTED CASH FLOW	CASH FLOW	DISCOUNTED CASH FLOW
0	(25 000 000)	(25 000 000)	(25 000 000)	(25 000 000)
1	6 000 000	5 660 400	6 000 000	5 660 400
2	7 000 000	6 230 000	6 000 000	5 340 000
3	7 000 000	5 877 200	6 000 000	5 037 600
4	7 500 000	5 940 750	6 000 000	4 752 600
5	7 500 000	5 604 750	6 000 000	4 483 800
Net present value		4 313 100		274 400

$$\text{Expected NPV} = (4\,313\,100 \times 0.8) + (274\,400 \times 0.2)$$
$$= £3\,505\,360$$

This particular case is quite clear. The RTS project has a higher ENPV and thus appears to be more attractive. However, it is worth reiterating one of the points made in the concluding section of Chapter 5. The ENPV value only tells us that, in the context of a large number of similar projects, there will be a propensity for the NPVs to tend, on aggregate, towards the value shown here. Thus, the ENPV is not, on its own, a reliable decision criterion for a specific case.

In the case of the alternatives being considered here, ENPV would be only one of many forms of analysis which would almost certainly involve sensitivity testing and simulation.

Table 6.7 RTS – Rapid Transit System

YEAR	Most likely scenario (operating at near capacity) Probability=0.65		Pessimistic scenario Probability=0.25	
	NET CASH FLOW	DISCOUNTED CASH FLOW	NET CASH FLOW	DISCOUNTED CASH FLOW
0	(22 000 000)	(22 000 000)	(22 000 000)	(22 000 000)
1	6 500 000	6 132 100	6 500 000	6 132 100
2	8 000 000	7 120 000	6 500 000	5 785 000
3	8 000 000	6 716 800	6 000 000	5 037 600
4	8 000 000	6 336 800	6 000 000	4 752 600
5	8 000 000	5 978 400	6 000 000	4 483 800
Net present value		10 284 100		4 191 100

$$\text{Expected NPV} = (10\ 284\ 100 \times 0.65) + (4\ 191\ 100 \times 0.25)$$
$$= £7\ 732\ 431$$

6.4 AN UNDERGROUND RAIL TUNNEL USING MERA

6.4.1 THE MERA TECHNIQUE

Multiple estimating using risk analysis (MERA)* is a technique for cost estimating developed by the, now privatized, Property Services Agency (a division of the UK Department of the Environment which was responsible for the design and procurement of government and military buildings). The technique is based on the principles of EMV as described in the example above and in Chapter 5. Use of MERA involves the production of three estimates: the base estimate (BE), the average risk estimate (ARE) and the maximum likely estimate (MLE). The base estimate, as you could guess, includes no explicit allowance for risk. The titles of the other two estimates are equally self-explanatory. The meanings of some other terms used in MERA are not so immediately obvious:

- **Risk allowance**   A sum of money allowed in an estimate to cover an item about which there is some uncertainty.
- **Fixed risk**   A risk which will either be incurred as a whole, with an estimated probability, or not at all. For example, if we are unsure about the exact location of the water table in a deep tunnelling operation, we know that after investigation we either will or will not need pumping equipment.
- **Variable risk**   A risk which can occur to a varying degree with varying probabilities of specific values in the range. For example, we know that the substructure construction for a multistorey building will depend on the ground conditions. It could thus vary from a very inexpensive design in good loadbearing conditions to a very expensive design if ground conditions are not favourable. Early in the process of project appraisal, before there are detailed site investigations, this can be described as a cost distribution.
- **Maximum risk allowance**   This is the sum of money to be allowed if the risk were to occur to its full extent.

---

*For information on MERA see Barnes (1989).

- **Maximum likely risk allowance**   For a variable risk this is, for practical purposes, the 'worst case', here defined as the case that would only have a 0.1 probability of being exceeded. For a fixed risk, the maximum likely risk allowance is the same as the maximum risk allowance.
- **Average risk allowance**   For fixed risks this is the EMV, the product of the size of the outcome and the probability of its occurrence. For variable risks the average risk allowance is the value which is estimated as having a 0.5 probability of being exceeded.
- **Spread**   The difference between the maximum likely and the average risk allowance.

The MERA technique consists of producing a conventional base estimate which is then accompanied by an average risk and a maximum risk estimate. The average risk estimate is produced by simple summation of the EMVs for all the fixed risks and 0.5 probability values for all the variable risk items. The maximum likely estimate is a summation of all the, effective, 'worst cases'. Simple summation of all the worst cases would produce an overly pessimistic result as the items should be reasonably independent and the chances of all worst cases occurring simultaneously should be very small. This has been discussed in Chapter 2. Therefore, the MLE is produced by statistically combining the maximum likely values and adding this to the base and the average risk values. The statistical combination is reached merely by squaring the spreads, summing these squares and then finding the square root of the sum. All of this is quite difficult to understand in the abstract and is better illustrated with an example. When you have worked through the example below it might be useful to re-read this paragraph in order to see the statement of the general case.

6.4.2   AN EXAMPLE OF THE MERA TECHNIQUE

This project is based on a real example, although the details have been altered for reasons of simplicity and professional confidentiality. The background is that we have been retained to advise the design team on costs at the preliminary stages of the project.

Table 6.8 Project: Rehabilitation of Underground Rail Tunnel

Location: Paris/R.E.R.
Currency: All figures converted to £ sterling at January 1993
Base estimate: = £4 000 000

RISK	PROBABILITY	AVERAGE RISK ALLOWANCE (£k)	MAXIMUM LIKELY RISK ALLOWANCE (£k)	SPREAD	(SPREAD)^2
Extent of relining (v)*		160	400	240	57 600
Special access provision (f)†	0.5	125	250	125	15 625
Additional waste disposal (v)		100	225	125	15 625
Revisions to brief (v)		90	225	135	18 225
Safety systems (f)	0.6	60	100	40	1 600
		535			108 675

*v=variable   †f=fixed

Risk estimate:
Base estimate   4 000 000   4 000 000
Average risk estimate   = 4 000 000 + 535 000   4 535 000
Maximum likely estimate   = 4 535 000 + √108 675   = 4 864 660
Average risk estimate   = 13.34% on base
Maximum likely estimate   = 21.62% on base

Detailed design work will commence within two months and the project is expected to start on site within two years. At this stage only preliminary surveys and site investigations have been carried out. There is a high degree of uncertainty about the full extent of relining that will be needed in the tunnel. At present there is a bill before the national parliament which, if enacted, will have a significant impact on safety measures needed to protect the operatives on the project. The City Planning Authority is still deliberating on the extent of disruption to road traffic that they will allow during the site work. There is a proposal that the contractors should be required to make special access provisions which involve temporary tunnels to avoid disruption to traffic. The final decision on this will not be made for another nine months as there is about to be an election for City Authority Representatives. At this point in the project the brief has not been fully developed and there is still some uncertainty about the extent of the work generally.

Against this background we are required to provide the Transport Authority with a probabilistic forecast which they can supply to their financiers, the Treasury Department. The MERA approach is adopted producing the figures shown in Table 6.8.

There are, it must be said, a number of criticisms of the MERA approach. First, it is mechanistic and rather inflexible. It is described in a rather procedural way, which does not encourage creative thought on the project. Nor does it encourage the project team to manage the risks, i.e. to do something about the results. Second, it only deals with costs. Third, it uses the EMV approach which has limitations, as described in Chapter 5. Fourth, it only deals with downside risks. Thus it could be responsible for producing very pessimistic, negative perceptions of projects. In summary, MERA is really a method of probabilistic estimating rather than a method of risk analysis which should be an integral component of risk management.

6.5 SOUTH CHINA LAND RECLAMATION

Shenzen is a Special Economic Zone in the province of Guangdong. Owing to buoyant economic growth, land availability along the coast is becoming more restricted. A land reclamation scheme is proposed to provide the space needed for a new container port and ancillary facilities.

Table 6.9 South China land reclamation

The lowest tender
Bills of Quantities
Summary

DESCRIPTION	MILLION Rmb
Bill No. 1 – Preliminaries	56.00
Bill No. 2 – Site clearance	0.30
Bill No. 3 – Roadworks	22.00
Bill No. 4 – Reclamation and sea walls	343.00
Bill No. 5 – Piers	152.00
Bill No. 6 – Pumphouse and pumping mains	64.00
Bill No. 7 – Drainage culverts	37.00
Bill No. 8 – Borrow areas	52.00
Bill No. 9 – Provisional sums and dayworks	30.00
Subtotal of bills 1 to 9 inclusive	756.30
Allowance for contract price fluctuation increase	50.00
Contingency sum	73.00
Total	879.30

6.5.1 PROJECT SCOPE

The project entails the reclamation of 250 hectares of land, the construction of sea walls, extension of existing culverts and the relocation of existing ferry piers.

The summary page of the lowest tender is shown in Table 6.9.

After a meeting between the client's team and the tenderer, bills 4 (Table 6.10) and 5 (Table 6.11) and the 'contingency' sum (Table 6.12) have been identified and agreed as three high-risk features which will need constant monitoring. Sensitivity testing was performed and results are tabulated as follows:

Table 6.10   Bill No. 4: Reclamation and sea walls

VARIATION	BILL SUBTOTAL (MILLION Rmb)	SUMMARY TOTAL (MILLION Rmb)
+50%	514.50	1050.80
+40%	480.20	1016.50
+30%	445.90	982.20
+20%	411.60	947.90
+10%	377.30	913.60
0	343.00	879.30
−10%	308.70	845.00
−20%	274.40	810.70
−30%	240.10	776.40
−40%	205.80	742.10
−50%	171.50	707.80

Table 6.11   Bill No. 5: Piers

VARIATION	BILL SUBTOTAL (MILLION Rmb)	SUMMARY TOTAL (MILLION Rmb)
+50%	228.00	955.30
+40%	212.80	940.10
+30%	197.60	924.90
+20%	182.40	909.70
+10%	167.20	894.50
0	152.00	879.30
−10%	136.80	864.10
−20%	121.60	848.90
−30%	106.40	833.70
−40%	91.20	818.50
−50%	76.00	803.30

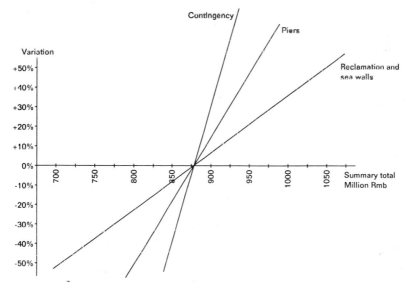

Figure 6.2 South China land reclamation: spider diagram

Table 6.12   Contingency sum

VARIATION	BILL SUBTOTAL (MILLION Rmb)	SUMMARY TOTAL (MILLION Rmb)
+50%	109.50	915.80
+40%	102.20	908.50
+30%	94.90	901.20
+20%	87.60	893.90
+10%	80.30	886.60
0	73.00	879.30
−10%	65.70	872.00
−20%	58.40	864.70
−30%	51.10	857.40
−40%	43.80	850.10
−50%	36.50	842.80

ANALYSIS

We are studying this project at the point where tenders have been received. By carrying out sensitivity tests on the most attractive bid we hope to minimize exposure to risk by identifying areas where our maximum project management efforts will be directed. In this case it is clear that the single most important part of the project, financially, is the 'reclamation and sea walls' package described in bill number 4.

A spider diagram (Figure 6.2) is used to illustrate the percentage change in project cost that is produced by changes to individual elements of the project.

Each line in the spider diagram indicates the impact, on the total cost, of a defined proportionate variation in a single parameter that has been identified as having some risk associated with its estimate. The flatter the line, the more sensitive will construction cost be to variation in that parameter. For example, it can be seen from the diagram that a variation in the estimate for 'reclamation and sea walls' would have a much greater impact on cost than an identical variation in 'piers' or 'contingency'.

6.6   A BRIDGE OVER THE THAMES

This case study is loosely based on a real project. It should, more accurately, be called 'A Bridge over Very Troubled Water'. In order to protect the innocent – and the guilty – the bridge has been moved from South East Asia to South London. The magnitude of the figures has been altered but their internal consistency has been retained. We have been retained as project managers for the preliminary appraisal and design phases of the project. We are required to advise the government department responsible on the finance necessary to procure the project. We have received the following approximate estimates from the design engineers.

We are specifically required to provide the Treasury with a probabilistic forecast of project cost.

Engineers' estimates at July 1993 in current prices

	£m
Contractor's design fee	2.50
Piling	25.50
Pile caps	2.75
Abutments	2.50
Precast beams and columns	50.00
Precast deck	10.00
Insitu concrete works	1.10
Pavements	5.00
Utilities and markings	1.00
Preliminaries	8.00

London Borough of Greenwich additional requirements

Access restrictions, noise restrictions, etc.	2.50
Uncharted utilities, diversions, etc.	2.00

We next spend an intensive two days with the team of design engineers, the result of which is the set of probabilistic forecasts for the various parts of the project shown in Table 6.13.

Table 6.13 Data Input – Project: Greenwich Bridge

ITEM	DESCRIPTION	DISTRIBUTION	LOWER	1ST BEST	2ND BEST	UPPER	OPERATOR
1	Contractor's design fee	Rectangular	2.50			3.00	+
2	Piling	Trapezoidal	25.00	30.00	32.00	38.00	+
3	Pile caps	Triangular	2.50	2.75		3.25	+
4	Abutments	Triangular	2.50	2.80		4.50	+
5	Precast beams/columns	Triangular	45.00	50.00		60.00	+
6	Precast deck	Trapezoidal	8.50	9.25	10.00	11.50	+
7	Insitu concrete work	Triangular	0.80	1.10		1.80	+
8	Pavements	Triangular	4.20	5.00		5.80	+
9	Utilities and markings	Rectangular	1.50			2.00	+
10	Preliminaries	Triangular	8.00	10.00		11.50	+
11	Additional requirements	Triangular	0.50	2.50		3.50	+
12	Uncharted utilities	Triangular	0.25	2.00		2.75	-
13	Fluctuation	Triangular	1.04	1.07		1.12	*

Table 6.14 Summary of simulation results – Project: Greenwich Bridge

BAND	BAND RANGE	FREQ.	CUM. FREQ.	BAND	BAND RANGE	FREQ.	CUM. FREQ.
1	105.30–107.30	0	0	16	135.31–137.31	97	871
2	107.30–109.30	0	0	17	137.31–139.31	65	936
3	109.30–111.30	0	0	18	139.31–141.31	44	980
4	111.30–113.30	0	0	19	141.31–143.31	10	990
5	113.30–115.30	0	0	20	143.31–145.31	8	998
6	115.30–117.30	0	0	21	145.31–147.31	2	1000
7	117.30–119.30	0	0	22	147.31–149.31	0	1000

#	Interval			#	Interval		
8	119.30–121.30	0	0	23	149.31–151.31	0	1000
9	121.30–123.30	13	13	24	151.31–153.31	0	1000
10	123.30–125.30	38	51	25	153.31–155.31	0	1000
11	125.30–127.30	83	134	26	155.31–157.31	0	1000
12	127.30–129.30	131	265	27	157.31–159.31	0	1000
13	129.30–131.31	170	435	28	159.31–161.31	0	1000
14	131.31–133.31	184	619	29	161.31–163.31	0	1000
15	133.31–135.31	155	774	30	163.31–165.31	0	1000

Range: 121.52–147.06

Mean: 132.17;   Standard deviation: 4.54

1st quartile: 128.30;   Median: 132.31;   3rd quartile: 134.31

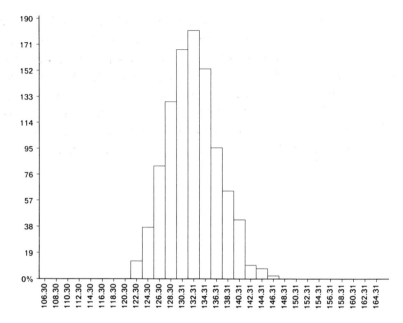

Figure 6.3   Greenwich Bridge: probability distribution

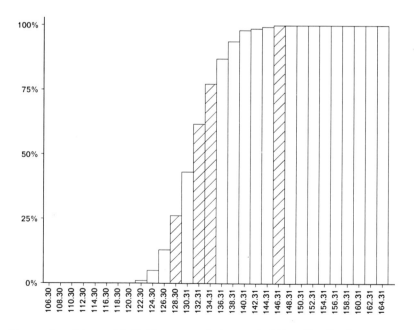

Figure 6.4   Greenwich Bridge: cumulative probability distribution

Once the Monte Carlo simulation process has been completed, the summary of simulation results can be tabulated (Table 6.14). The cumulative density distribution and probability density distribution histograms are drawn as shown (Figures 6.3 and 6.4). We can now tell the financier that the estimate of the construction cost for the bridge will be £132 million and the standard deviation is £4.34 million. Additionally we can report that there is a 75% chance of getting the bridge at the cost of £134.31 million or less.

CHAPTER 7

SOFTWARE FOR RISK ANALYSIS

7.1 INTRODUCTION

In this chapter we shall assess the role of software and provide some advice on how to approach the software market. The type of product available will be described in general terms. We wish here to orient the reader, not to provide detailed assessments of particular products.

7.2 THE ROLE OF SOFTWARE IN RISK ANALYSIS

Software plays an important but minor part in the overall process of risk analysis and risk management. It is not practically possible to carry out a simulation of most projects without access to software. Yet, the number-crunching part of the simulation may well be the least important part of the total time spent dealing with the identification, analysis and management of project risks. **Thus, risk analysis software is not sufficient and may not even be necessary for good risk management.**

Computer software will not play any significant part in the identification of project and external risks. This identification process is lengthy and creative. It relies on well-trained, highly experienced human experts who are able to think creatively and imaginatively about the range and likelihood of future outcomes attached to a wide variety of events related to the project and its political and economic environment. The software will play no role in helping the decision maker to assess the corporate attitude to the risk exposure which may have been quantified as a result of the analysis.

There will frequently be situations where formal risk management is practised but the management never reaches the stage of doing a quantified analysis. A thorough risk identification stage may lead to the generation of sufficient information for the decision makers to take action without a formal quantified analysis.

The software will play little or no role in the formulation of strategies for response to the circumstances which can be envisaged at the time of planning or carrying out the analysis. The only vital ingredient that is absolutely necessary for the good practice of construction risk analysis and management is the appropriate attitude of mind, being accustomed to thinking probabilistically about the plans and assumptions underlying construction project forecasts and project management.

It is nevertheless necessary to have some software product available for use in the situations where a quantified analysis is appropriate. Software will undoubtedly be necessary in order to carry out routine simulation of project estimates.

7.3   HOW TO APPROACH THE SOFTWARE MARKET

The important criterion is to consider where the maximum benefit lies. This will not necessarily be correlated to the price paid for the software tools. There are four approaches to the purchase of software in this, as in most, fields.

The first is a custom-designed product. This custom-designed approach ensures that the software fits into the in-house project management system.

The second approach to the market is to consider the purchase of relatively cheap add-ons to spreadsheet programs. These usually cost of the order of £100 to £300 per user. Clearly they rely on the user already having a spreadsheet program running. An example of this is the program known as @ Risk which links to Lotus 123.

The third approach is to look at the relatively large off-the-shelf packages. These are usually based around project management suites, such as those from ARTEMIS and PRIMAVERA. These programs are extremely powerful project management packages. The add-ons usually enable the user to make probabilistic inputs to the network activities, which means that they will deal with both time and cost. These programs may cost something of the order of around £1000 per user and they rely on the relevant project management system already being in place. ARTEMIS, for example, costs around £3500 at present. The disadvantage of these programs is that they are complicated to use, partly because they are so powerful. Often they require that the project be set up as a critical path network. This is suitable for certain types of work;

for example, a firm or client who deals with a relatively small number of very large projects. Off-shore oil and gas rigs and petrochemical installations are examples of the latter.

The fourth approach is to consider a software product – which may be stand-alone or may double as a project management tool similar to those mentioned – which emanates from a consultant who specializes in risk, rather than in software or project management sales. There are at least two packages of this type available in the market at present. These packages tend to be relatively expensive (of the order of £5000). They are usually accompanied by specific training in risk management, which may bring the total costs to the order of £10 000.

7.3.1 The market for risk analysis software

The market for risk analysis is a niche market. It is small and specialized. There are a number of products which, although they appear in software users' guides, have been withdrawn from the market. This is frequently because risk analysis is a field which requires significant training and support. Many software houses find this too specialized to be economic. Some risk analysis products have been brought to the market before they were sufficiently well developed, and this has resulted in their being withdrawn altogether. A high value added area is where the tool is being marketed by a firm which specializes in risk consultancy rather than software sales. These latter products tend to be excellent, and expensive.

Much good work in risk analysis and risk management can be done with very basic and inexpensive software accompanied by a thorough training of the relevant staff. Expense will start to be incurred if there is a requirement to ensure that the risk tool produces standardized departmental reports which communicate with information in your firm's own management or information system.

7.4   CRITERIA FOR THE ASSESSMENT OF SOFTWARE

Large continuing clients may feel that they deal with a relatively large number of projects, many of which are, relatively small and routine. It may be the case that major risk lies in the potential accumulation of insufficient/excessive risk allowances across a large number of small projects. In general, the greater the degree of functionality in the software, the more expensive and less friendly it becomes. Each product attempts to make its own compromise on this. Most products will support a wide range of distributions – usually far in excess of normal requirements. Some of the larger critical path network-based products support 'conditional branching', which is a method of dealing with correlation, described in Chapter 5 as follows:

> Correlation may be dealt with in this manner. Assume that activity P is dependent on the outcome of an earlier activity, say, activity K. The program should allow for this to be flagged when entering the basic simulation model. For activity P a number of different distributions are entered, each one contingent upon a specific type of result from activity K. Now, in the simulation when it is time to draw a number for activity P, the program checks back to read the result drawn for activity K during the same pass. Reading this result the program then decides which of the range of distributions for P is now appropriate, given the outcome of activity K. For example, the results of K could be banded into three different sections. A lower band producing a very optimistic result, a middle band and a higher band producing a pessimistic result. In this case we could enter three distributions to activity P, one for each of the three cases. The correlation may be positive, where a good result in K implies a good result in P, or negative, where a good result in K implies a bad result in P.

Clearly, conditional branching is one of the indicators of a top-quality software product in this field. It should be noted, though, that having access to the functionality of conditional branching requires that the user has quite a sophisticated understanding of the issues surrounding the correlation between sources of risk. There is a useful analogy here with placing a high-powered motor car in the hands of a novice driver. The driver may get from A to B more quickly, and in one piece, in a smaller, more appropriate vehicle.

CHAPTER 8

GOOD PRACTICE IN RISK MANAGEMENT

8.1 INTRODUCTION

This chapter is not intended to be a summary of the book. Instead, we shall partly restate our initial objectives and remind ourselves of the focus of the book before gathering together some practical ideas which should help readers to think constructively and clearly about how to identify, analyse and react to project risks. The information given in this chapter will only be useful on condition that the reader has reflected on the material presented throughout the book and has developed an understanding of risks and how to handle them.

One of the key objectives of this book has been to demonstrate that risk analysis cannot be mechanized, that software by itself is not the solution, and that the most important characteristic needed to analyse and manage risk is an appropriate frame of mind. Throughout the text we have been encouraging the reader to think about project risks and the human context in which we make judgements about them. When we assess probabilities we make decisions about future events based on our professional experience, simple rules of thumb and our knowledge of how humans perceive and model risks. Into each analysis is fed a series of data, assumptions, judgements and prejudices; therefore, we need to treat the entire process with caution and common sense. Accordingly, the remainder of this chapter has been organized into three sections:

- a section which addresses some human factors in risk analysis management
- a summary of key points of good practice in risk management
- some overall conclusions.

8.2 HUMAN FACTORS

Although this is a very short book, we have covered a lot of ground. We began with an exploration of the meaning of risk and uncertainty and a review of uncertainty in forecasts of construction prices and times. We then considered probability as a representation of expert judgement about future events. In Chapter 3 we looked at psychological aspects of forecasting construction prices, focusing in particular on errors and biases. In Chapter 4 we considered the range of human attitudes to risk. In Chapters 5, 6 and 7 we described and presented a range of techniques for risk analysis and probabilistic modelling.

While not wanting to devalue your work in reading this material – or my work in writing it – it is important to say that although all of the above is necessary, it is not **sufficient** to achieve competent practice in risk management. The final piece of the jigsaw is the human being. Readers who have worked through the text should have the technical knowledge necessary to carry out the analysis. More importantly, they should have developed frameworks for approaching projects in terms of their risks and for embarking on what has been called 'the dialog necessary for discovery' (Krantz, 1992). The discovery we are referring to is a realistic perception of the project with its range and relative likelihood of outcomes. Achieving this involves gaining a clear understanding of human perceptions of projects and risks and uncertainties. The technical details described in the previous paragraph all exist in the context of people working in organizations. It is to this that we now turn. In assembling the material for the remaining paragraphs I have relied heavily on an excellent seminar paper by Laurence Krantz of Eurolog, a specialist risk management consultancy (Krantz, 1992).

Let me preface this paragraph by saying that what follows is nothing more than common sense. Human factors in the minutiae of risk attitudes, subjective assessments of probabilities and biases are not the concern of this section. Here we are concerned with the behavioural and organizational context of the project. Frequently there are two sets of opposing forces in place in the human context of a project risk analysis. On the one hand, the person responsible for leading the risk analysis (whether he or she is a member of the team or an outside consultant) needs to be aware that people often 'fall in love' with their projects. This carries with it, the implication that the project team may not be receptive to the whole process of risk identification, analysis and management. If we are lucky enough to have a risk analyst laden with social and interpersonal skills who manages to 'sell' the idea to the project team, we may then find ourselves confronting the opposing force of negative attitudes which sometimes ensue from an improperly conducted risk analysis. The key problem is obvious: to navigate a path through these two extremes.

In order to navigate this path successfully, two things are necessary. First, it is necessary to ensure that there is a firm and open-minded commitment to the analysis from senior levels in the organization. Without this, the only possibility of a successful outcome to the analysis will be by good luck. The analyst needs to be clearly briefed on exactly what decisions remain to be taken and on the expectations that the organization holds for the risk analysis. Second, the risk analysis should have a positive outcome. It should not result in gloom and negative attitudes about the project. It should result in everyone gaining a more complete and a more realistic view of the project and its future. The positive feature of this is that it provides the opportunity for learning about the project in order to achieve a maturity of judgement in subsequent project decisions. The objective is not to replace engineering judgement with analysis, but to enable judgements to be made on the basis of more realistic information.

8.3 KEY POINTS OF GOOD PRACTICE

Project appraisal of the project appraisal. . .
Before doing any work, carry out an investment appraisal. How big is the project? How much of my time, and theirs, should be spent? Often there will be no need for a detailed and expensive risk analysis; sometimes there will. What is important is to discover which category you are in before you start work.

Nothing to fear. . .
There is no need for excessive fear. Remember the quote at the beginning of Chapter 1

Surprise them, be positive. . .
People may expect a risk analysis to be a rather gloomy and negative affair. Remember that the point of the exercise is to

present positive suggestions about how to deal with the project. If your analysis is framed in such a way that this is not feasible, then you are not doing it right.

Support from above...

In order to make things happen you need the cooperation of the team and the client organization, which may be your own employer. Therefore, you need to have commitment from the team and from senior people in the organization.

Reinforce common sense...

Remember that the objective is not to replace judgement but to enable it to be more fully informed with high-quality, realistic perceptions of project outcomes.

A structure for the process...

There is no prescription for how to do risk management, each case will be different. This is why this book has been written in its present form. Most cases will, however, include the following activities.

- *Structuring the problem*   What, exactly, does the client/team want? What is the nature of the project? What are its principal components? Who are the stakeholders?
- *Identification of risks*   Sounds easy, but a formal technique, such as brainstorming, may help to elicit complete information. Arrange the risks into reasonably independent groups for the purposes of analysis.
- *Assessment of probabilities*   Use more than one person if possible. Cross-check items with different people. Look for inconsistencies. Ask the same question in different ways. If you find inconsistencies, be happy. Feeding them back to the team will help everyone to learn more about the project.
- *Analysis*   Use whatever technique(s) you consider appropriate.
- *Interpretation of results*   Remember what the client has requested. Be able to make positive suggestions.

8.4 CONCLUSIONS

Techniques are necessary but not sufficient. Mechanistic, checklist approaches to risk analysis have limitations. In this book we have focused on developing a framework for approaching all projects, large and small, in a way which encourages realistic practical assessment of risks. Recognizing the role of people and their experiences and perceptions in framing designs and project decisions lifts risk analysis beyond a mere technical procedure. People and their biases and inconsistencies should not be treated as an obstacle to analysis; they are, instead, a resource which can be used to gain a mature expert understanding of the project.

One of the principal advantages of the thing we call risk analysis is that it helps people to make better-informed decisions.

REFERENCES

Barnes, M. (1989) Introducing MERA. *Chartered Quantity Surveyor*, January, p. 19.

Chapman, C.B. (1991) Risk, in *Investment, Procurement and Performance in Construction* (eds P. Venmore-Rowland, P. Brandon and T. Mole), E. & F.N. Spon (Chapman & Hall), London, pp. 259–75.

Hayes, R.W., Perry, J.G., Thompson, P.A. and Willmer, G. (1986) *Risk Management in Engineering Construction*, Thomas Telford, London.

Krantz, L. (1992) So you've been told to do a project risk audit. Seminar on risk, delivered at *Project Management North 92*, 12 November 1992, New Century Hall, Manchester.

Ruegg, R.T. and Marshall, H.E. (1990) *Building Economics: Theory and Practice*, Van Nostrand Reinhold, New York.

Marshall, H.E. (1991) *Economic Methods and Risk Analysis Techniques for Evaluating Building Investments: A Survey*, Report 136, International Council for Building Research Studies and Documentation, Rotterdam.

FURTHER READING

Byrne, P. and Cadman, D. (1984) *Risk, Uncertainty and Decision Making in Property Development*, E. & F.N. Spon (Chapman & Hall) London.

Cooper, D.F. and Chapman, C.B. (1987) *Risk Analysis for Large Projects: Models, Methods and Cases*, Wiley, New York.

Hertz, D.B. and Thomas, H. (1983) *Risk Analysis and its Applications*, Wiley, New York.

Pouliquen, L.Y. (1970) *Risk Analysis in Project Appraisal*, World Bank Staff, Occasional Paper, The Johns Hopkins Press, Baltimore.

INDEX

LIVERPOOL JOHN MOORES UNIVERSITY
Aldham Roberts L.R.C.
TEL. 051 231 3701/3634